Governance Reconsidered

Susan Resneck Pierce

Governance Reconsidered

How Boards, Presidents, Administrators, and Faculty Can Help Their Colleges Thrive

insidehighered.com

A Wiley Brand

The Jossey-Bass Higher and Adult Education Series

Library of Congress Cataloging-in-Publication Data
Library of Congress Cataloging-in-Publication Data has been applied for and is on file with the Library of Congress.
ISBN 978-1-1187-3849-8 (cloth)
ISBN 978-1-118-73862-7 (ebk.)
ISBN 978-1-118-73857-3 (ebk.)

Printed in the United States of America
FIRST EDITION
HB Printing 10 9 8 7 6 5 4 3 2 1

Contents

For my father, Elliott Resneck

For my sisters, Linda Resneck DiStefano Krohn and Brenda Resneck Laughery

For my daughter and son-in law, Sasha and Steven Seigel

For my grandsons, Sean and Ryan Siegel

Foreword

Dr. Susan Resneck Pierce is the celebrated former president of the University of Puget Sound and the author of *On Being Presidential*, one of the preeminent guides for college and university leaders. With this second contribution, *Governance Reconsidered*, to the canon of the American academy, she is becoming one of the most consequential scholars of the discipline of higher education. Without leaving anything to the imagination, she inspires the imagination. She writes with clarity and specificity and provides examples and case studies which one can actually use to address a working agenda.

University presidents are burning out like so many moths in a room filled with lit candles. *Governance Reconsidered* provides an antidote to this melancholy circumstance. To read this book is to experience the scales falling from one's eyes about the management and governance of America's colleges and universities in one of the most daunting times since the Great Depression. Pierce has identified the most significant contemporary challenges to institutions of higher education and their leaders and has provided answers that are insightful and informed by reflection and practice. In her studies she covers shared governance, university financing, university personnel issues, the place of the university in America, and remarkable and fascinating tales of issues addressed by presidents, faculty, and trustees. This book is a tool that will help institutions address their future.

This book will be of interest to all who have any concern whatsoever with the future of our nation's colleges and universities. It will be particularly helpful to policy makers and practitioners and should be read by political leaders, university presidents, and other administrators, including provosts, vice presidents, deans, and department chairs. Faculty who need to be knowledgeable about the institutions which host their work will also benefit from this valuable volume; likewise, students of both university administration and governance. Every trustee of state-supported and independent colleges and universities should receive a copy of this book along with his or her appointment letter. Journalists and others who think and write about the academy should have this on their desk to consult on a regular basis. Parents sending their youngsters off to college, as well as adult learners, should read this volume in order to better understand the institutions with which they are engaged. In other words, this is an important book, perhaps vital, for all.

Someone who reads *Governance Reconsidered* as well as *On Being Presidential* will begin to understand the fascinating special world of the American university. The literature will reveal how universities work and don't; will describe generic and unique challenges of university leadership; and will give reason for concern and encouragement. But Pierce's contribution is surely one of the most contemporary and comprehensive available and should be at the top of any such reading list. It is an outstanding contribution and, properly understood and used, will save the career of many a university leader in the demanding days to come.

At age seventy-six, I have not lived long enough to completely understand the meaning of the term "shared governance" as it is applied to colleges and universities and yet it persists, as I have myself said elsewhere, to enjoy an almost religious status in the academy, even while the tempo of faculty deliberations goes on to dominate university decision making. This is as true today as it was one, two, or three decades ago, even as we engage now in an even more taxing environment where large amounts of money are committed and the strategic agenda is increasingly complicated.

The culture of faculty tends to be risk adverse. This is arguably the result of the skill set developed while earning a PhD where the credential was not historically awarded for pyrotechnics. It is hard to recall when the need for sound decisions made in a timely manner was more imperative on campus, and yet our universities have divided into what the late C. P. Snow called, "two cultures"—one of which focuses on decision making while the other makes decisions. And if the second group doesn't apply themselves, then the first may have cause to worry about future compensation and employment. This is not a good thing. Susan Resneck Pierce's book addresses and helps to mitigate the worst concerns that I contemplate. She explains why shared governance must be accompanied by shared responsibility. She illustrates that fiscal concerns involving big data needs full-time attention that is not an easy fit with full-time scholarship and teaching. She shows why when these two cultures come together the meeting is sometimes noisy. The deliberate faculty culture may not fully appreciate that shared governance includes a timely call to action; and that universities are about to be disrupted, as have most recently journalism, medical care, and other historic practices. The reconciliation of faculty and administrators to the common good within the process of vital decision making could not be more imperative. President Pierce's contribution is the right book at the right time.

Stephen Joel Trachtenberg

Stephen Joel Trachtenberg is President Emeritus and University Professor of Public Service at The George Washington University. He is the author of five books about higher education, most recently along with Gerald B. Kauvar and E. Grady Bogue, of Presidencies Derailed: Why University Leaders Fail and How to Prevent It *(Johns Hopkins University Press).*

Preface

In July 1984, two weeks after I began what turned out to be a six-year tenure as the dean of the College of Arts and Sciences at the University of Tulsa, the provost, Thomas F. Staley, gave me important advice. Telling me that I was off to a good start, he cautioned that I might be even more effective if I were a bit more patient. Specifically, he advised me to look both ways before crossing the street.

As dean, I was in the enviable position of being an administrator with no financial worries. Tulsa's enrollment was about 4,000 students. The endowment was around $450 million. Tom had dedicated $250,000 annually for an arts and sciences discretionary fund to be used to enhance our academic programs. The only technology that we really worried about populated our science and language laboratories, and those labs were well equipped. No one seriously questioned the value of higher education. Those days are long gone, even at Tulsa.

At the beginning of that fall term, I constituted the department chairs as an advisory council. They had not previously met as a group and so were skeptical about whether these twice-monthly meetings would have value. In response, I told the department chairs that I wanted them to advise me on matters of importance to the college. I expressed the hope that together we might be able to make decisions that would benefit teaching and learning and that also would make a difference for our colleagues and our students.

At our first meeting, I asked the department chairs about the unusual policy that all arts and sciences graduates, including those majoring in fields like biology and mathematics, received Bachelor of Arts degrees. The department chairs unanimously agreed that we should also offer the Bachelor of Science degree. We quickly agreed on which degrees belonged in the arts category and which in the sciences.

I suggested that the department chairs each discuss the matter with their departmental colleagues and report back at our next meeting in two weeks. If, as we now all anticipated, there was broad agreement, we could simply make the change. The provost and president had already agreed it was a good idea. We would not need to take the matter to the board.

One department chair, ignoring my proposed timetable, mused that making this change, which he favored, would take a long time. When I asked him how long, he responded, "At least three years." I, not having yet mastered the art of patience, exclaimed, "Why three years?" He then asked how long I thought it would take. I said that I was thinking about something like three days but that I could live with three weeks. We did make the change in two weeks.

There was in fact no real urgency to changing a policy that had apparently existed for many decades, and the impetus for seeking action within two weeks was not impatience. Rather, I hoped to demonstrate to my new colleagues that with appropriate consultation and communication, we could make and implement obvious decisions easily and quickly. These colleagues and many others on the faculty became supportive of that approach, and over the next several years, through their collaborative and creative efforts, we earned a Phi Beta Kappa chapter, began to internationalize our offerings, created partnerships with such cultural organizations as Tulsa Opera, increased enrollment, improved student quality, and earned grants from national foundations.

The Inspiration for This Book

My interest in the topic of governance has been inspired both by recent changes in the higher education landscape and by my work since 1973 as a faculty member, a department chair, a dean, an academic vice president, a president, a member of a number of nonprofit boards, and, for the past eight years, a consultant. The many conversations I have had in my consulting role with faculty members, administrators, students, trustees, alumni, leaders of higher education associations and foundations, and elected officials have informed my thinking about governance in new and more nuanced ways.

In the past several years, new economic and political pressures, along with the advent of new technologies, have led to conflicts on many campuses over who is responsible for the nature and pace of change generally and for decisions about academic matters in particular. On these campuses, contentiousness has often replaced collaboration.

Concerns about ever-growing expenses and ever-increasing tuition, for example, have led some governors and other elected officials to seek in unprecedented ways to influence the leadership, the curriculum, the tuition, and even the conventional classroom-based approach to teaching at a number of state-supported universities. These same concerns have led boards of both public and private colleges and universities to push presidents to make changes quickly to eliminate programs and even positions that are not cost-effective and to identify and implement new revenue streams. Many presidents have done just that, turning to the academic programs, which until recently on many campuses had been protected from budget cuts and which previously had been considered the province of the faculty. Having already made all the cuts that they believed that they could make in nonacademic areas, many presidents and their senior administrative colleagues have phased out academic programs and hired adjuncts rather than tenure-track faculty to meet instructional needs. Many presidents have also led their institution to add new majors (often pre-professional) and new graduate programs, to create online courses often taught by adjuncts, to enroll greater numbers of international students, or to establish campuses abroad.

When presidents and their senior colleagues take such actions without honoring the often time-consuming, highly deliberative processes of shared governance, they almost always trigger conflict with the faculty, who inevitably value those processes and their deliberative nature. In such instances, faculty members typically argue that shared governance as it has historically been practiced ensures that all academic decisions are mission-driven and that all academic programs are of high quality. Higher education journals and the national press are now filled with stories about faculty members at both public and private colleges and universities who are critical of their presidents and sometimes their boards for making unilateral, top-down decisions that faculty members maintain have compromised academic values and academic quality.

This book will specifically explore how and why the notion of shared governance as it has been practiced to varying degrees on most US campuses since the mid-1960s is being challenged and even shattered on many campuses. The book will describe how conflicts about governance often escalate in ways that are destructive to the institutions about which trustees, presidents, and faculty generally care so deeply. Finally, the book will reconsider governance, offering recommendations to trustees, presidents, and faculty members about their roles and responsibilities going forward so that they can enable their institutions to thrive and in some cases to survive.

The Intended Audience

This book is intended for trustees, presidents, senior administrators, faculty members, elected officials, leaders of higher education associations and foundations, and people who care about the quality of higher education in this country. I hope to help those in each group to understand the roles and responsibilities of each of the players and the complexities inherent in those responsibilities. I also hope to inspire them to work together effectively rather than to be locked in adversarial relationships that harm our colleges and universities and inevitably their students as well.

The Structure of This Book

Chapter 1 begins with a history of shared governance in the United States and the challenges it has faced historically and currently faces. In writing this chapter, I was particularly struck by how the American Association of University Professors (AAUP) was at its founding a century ago focused primarily on the question of academic freedom and that only in its 1966 statement did the AAUP make explicit the linkage of shared governance and academic freedom. This chapter also discusses the impact on the presidency of contentiousness on many campuses about governance.

Chapter 2 focuses on the causes of the various financial pressures facing colleges and universities today and explores the impact of constrained resources not only on the quality of the academic programs but increasingly on how governance is practiced and, on a number of campuses, has been shattered.

Chapter 3 describes the growing reliance on contingent faculty, the vast majority of whom are part-time and who do not participate in governance. This chapter further explores the similarly negative implications for shared governance of MOOCs (massive open online courses), online learning, and for-profit institutions.

Chapter 4 considers the impact on governance of growing questions about the value and cost of higher education. Specifically, the chapter explores ways in which higher education is in fact vulnerable to some of the criticism it is receiving from elected officials, commentators on higher education, and trustees. The chapter also makes the case for the value of a college education and describes the negative effect of elected officials and trustees substituting their judgment for that of college and university presidents in terms of policy and budget and for that of the faculty in terms of curriculum and other academic matters.

Chapters 5, 6, and 7 offer cautionary tales about presidential, faculty, and trustee actions respectively. Each chapter also offers recommendations for how each of these groups need to reconsider governance and work together collaboratively so that their institutions will thrive and in some cases simply survive.

The book ends on a more hopeful note by presenting, in chapter 8, four exemplary tales about presidents who have been responsible for bringing about transformational change on their campuses and who have done so in partnership with the faculty and the board. Each of these mini-case studies highlights the benefits of presidents who successfully engage their campuses and their trustees in thinking about and contributing ideas for how their institutions can most productively move forward.

Some Explanations for My Readers

I draw heavily throughout the book on examples of both dysfunctional and effective governance.

When these examples have made their way into the national press and also social media and have received extensive coverage, I name the institutions and cite that coverage as I think appropriate. I am aware that such accounts, whether in the mainstream press, blogs, or Facebook posts, may be incomplete, biased, or both. (Although I make every attempt to present these stories fairly, as a student of William Faulkner's fiction, I am mindful of the unreliability of narratives and so recognize that those who are closer to the events that I am recounting than I am may have different understandings and perspectives about those events.)

When I know of examples that, to the institution's good fortune, have not made their way into the public realm, I seek to disguise the institution and the players. In such cases, I sometimes change the gender of the president, trustees, or key faculty members. I sometimes describe the institution as being located in a different setting. I sometimes modestly alter the institution's mission. I sometimes alter slightly the details of events. And in a few cases I conflate similar events that have occurred on two campuses into one case study. At the same time, I want to be clear that the stories I tell are always grounded in real events.

I have learned about these examples in a number of ways. Sometimes, I simply have firsthand knowledge. Sometimes, the stories have come to me from those on the campus itself. In all instances when there is contentiousness, I have sought to understand and represent all sides of the issue.

I also want to point out some choices about terminology. Although members of governing boards at public institutions are often referred to as "regents," for the sake of simplicity and to emphasize that governing boards are entrusted with the health and integrity of their institution, I will use the term *trustees* throughout the book. Similarly, although the chief executive officer on some campuses is referred to as the chancellor, I have chosen throughout to use the more common title of *president*.

Finally, because Jossey-Bass prefers not to use footnotes or endnotes, I am including an extended bibliography that lists the numerous newspaper and journal articles that have provided me with pertinent information.

Acknowledgments

After my interview in February 1992 as a finalist for the presidency of the University of Puget Sound, I arrived home just in time to receive a phone call from the board and search committee chair, the quite wonderful late Lowry Wyatt, who offered me the position. I accepted without asking about the salary. We agreed to meet two days later to talk about details. I hung up the phone, and before I called my family and friends to share the good news, I danced around my house.

That moment was the last time I failed to negotiate vigorously, although going forward my negotiations were for the college, not for me personally. It was also the last time that I danced alone, because I quickly learned that creating partnerships with my colleagues, trustees, students, alumni, the community, national foundations, and others would better serve Puget Sound than any solo act I might pull off.

Although the early sections of this book include cautionary tales about boards, presidents, and members of the faculty who have contributed to or even created dysfunction on their campus, I want to emphasize that I nevertheless have a deep and abiding faith in this country's colleges and universities.

The great majority of faculty members with whom I have worked have been dedicated to their students. These faculty members have sought to teach students to be critical thinkers, to write and speak clearly, to value logical arguments supported by evidence, and to be passionate about ideas and knowledge. Over and over again, I have seen faculty members who have been transforming agents—in the most positive of ways—in the lives of their students. Although I certainly have encountered my share of criticism, recalcitrance, and political posturing from some faculty members, I have also and always (please note that I said "always") been able to count on the collective wisdom of my faculty colleagues when it came to institutional matters.

Similarly, I have also come to know some unbelievably effective presidents who have brought about constructive change on their campuses in collaboration with the faculty and with the support of their boards. They have much to teach us about effective leadership, and so I will try to point out throughout the book the lessons to be learned from them. In particular, I want to thank Francesco Cesareo, Assumption College; Tom Evans, Carroll College; Mark Gordon, Defiance College; Rob Huntington, Heidelberg University; Rock Jones, Ohio Wesleyan University; Steve Kaplan, University of New Haven; Brit Kirwan, the University of Maryland System; Ted Long, Elizabethtown College; Bob McMahan, Kettering University; Vince Maniaci, American International College: Jo Ellen Parker, Sweet Briar College; Georgia Nugent, Kenyon College; Pam Reid, the University of St. Joseph; Steve Trachtenberg, George Washington University; and Rich Wagner, Dunwoody College of Technology. In addition, I want to acknowledge two provosts who have also taught me a great deal: Bob Entzminger, Hendrix College, and Patricia Killen, Gonzaga University.

I have also worked with some exemplary trustees. Although there are too many to name, I especially want to thank Bill Weyerhaeuser, my board chair for ten of my eleven years at Puget Sound; Terry Lengfelder, the board's vice chair; and trustee Hal Eastman, each of whom encouraged me to think in strategic ways and to act boldly. I further want to acknowledge some of the current and former board chairs and vice chairs with whom I have been fortunate to work:

Fred Bayon, Assumption College; Richard Willis and Ray Murff of Baylor University; Ray Messer, Mark Semmons, and Terry Cosgrove of Carroll College (Montana); Phil Mallott of Defiance College; Maurice Wagener and Ted Ferrara, Dunwoody College of Technology; Kathleen McKinney and Rich Cullen of Furman University; Sondra Libman of Heidelberg University; Charlie Kettering of Kettering University; Kathe Rhinesmith and Michael Long of Ohio Wesleyan University; and Virginia Upchurch Collier and Elisabeth Wyatt, Sweet Briar College.

I am again grateful to my editor, David Brightman, executive editor for Higher and Adult Education at Jossey-Bass. (OK, I admit it: I love to say the phrase "my editor.") I first worked with David on my recent book, *On Being Presidential: A Guide for Colleges and Universities*, and suddenly understood the enormous value a truly talented editor brings to a manuscript. In the case of this book, David wisely encouraged me to expand my interest in writing a book about trusteeship to the larger question of governance. It was he who suggested the book's title, with its nod to the much-admired Ernie Boyer's pathbreaking work *Scholarship Reconsidered*. David is a consummate editor and a good friend.

I also deeply appreciate the support of Aneesa Davenport, associate marketing manager for Higher and Adult Education at Jossey-Bass, and Cathy Cambron for her superb copyediting.

And I continue to be indebted to Scott Jacshik, editor at and cofounder of *Inside Higher Ed*, first for encouraging me to write for *IHE*, then for introducing me to David Brightman and Jossey-Bass, next for sponsoring *On Being Presidential*, and now for sponsoring *Governance Reconsidered*.

Writing is very solitary and demanding work. In that light, I want to thank my friends Karen Goldstein and Joel Trosch and my daughter, Alexandra (Sasha) Siegel, for being avid and critical readers of various iterations of this manuscript. They each gave me, in different ways, the kind of encouragement I needed to write the book and the critical perspective that led me to make it better.

I want to thank my grandsons, Sean and Ryan Siegel (ten and eight at this writing), for providing me almost daily with a much-needed respite from writing. They also have become my biggest promoters. For instance, while waiting for pizza to be served one evening at a local restaurant, they found *On Being Presidential* on Amazon.com. They proudly showed the website to the waitress and waiter and to everyone sitting near us. Each of them is a voracious reader, and they are better writers at their respective ages than I ever was. How lucky am I?

I also want to acknowledge my 93-year-old father, who remains deeply interested in my work; my sisters, Linda Resneck DiStefano Krohn and Brenda Resneck Laughery, who simply give me support no matter what; and my son-in-law, Steven Siegel, who makes me happy because he so loves my daughter and my grandchildren. I also want to thank Albert (Bert) Sonnenfeld, who has been an important part of my life since he was the best teacher I ever had when I was a graduate student, and John Riggs, who has been a friend since we were teenagers in Janesville, Wisconsin, some decades ago. And although my husband, Kenneth Pierce, died almost seven years ago, his insights into how institutions work and his unfailing encouragement still inspire me.

Finally, I want to acknowledge a number of my former students throughout my career as a faculty member and administrator. That I am still in touch with each of them makes me happy. By virtue of who they have become and the ways they each have made a difference in the lives of others, they make me proud and reaffirm my faith in higher education.

About the Author

As soon as Susan Resneck Pierce stepped down after eleven years (1992–2003) as the president of the University of Puget Sound, she began "flunking retirement." Today, as president of SRP CONSULTING, LLC, she advises colleges and universities on such matters as effective board and presidential performance, governance, board development, and strategic planning. She serves as a coach to presidents and an advisor to board chairs. She often facilitates focused retreats for boards, senior administrators, and faculty. Dr. Pierce also serves "Of Counsel" to Witt-Kieffer and, as a member of its Education Leadership Council, advises the firm about trends in higher education.

Dr. Pierce writes and speaks extensively about higher education. Her book *On Being Presidential: A Guide for College and University Leaders* (Jossey-Bass, 2011), like this book, is sponsored by *Inside Higher Ed*, to which she is a frequent contributor. She is also the author of *The Moral of the Story* (Columbia University's Teachers College Press, 1982), coeditor of a book on Ralph Ellison's *Invisible Man*, and author of many essays about American literature. In recent years, she has given presentations at meetings sponsored by the American Council on Education, the American Council of Academic Deans, the Council of Independent Colleges (CIC), the National Association of Colleges and Universities, and the National Association for Student Affairs Administrators in Higher Education.

Under Dr. Pierce's leadership, the University of Puget Sound entered the ranks of the national liberal arts colleges. As the result of a successful comprehensive campaign and a careful use of institutional resources, the endowment grew from $68 million to $213 million; the college completed $85 million of new construction and major renovations; SAT scores increased from 1067 to 1253; and applications for 650 freshmen places grew to number 4,400 annually. To honor President Emerita Pierce's work at Puget Sound, donors endowed both a chair in humanities and honors and a lecture series in public affairs and the arts in her name. In addition, thanks also to a major donor, the atrium of Puget Sound's new humanities building also carries her name.

From 1990 to 1992 Dr. Pierce served as vice president for academic affairs at Lewis & Clark College and from 1984 to 1990 as dean of the College of Arts and Sciences at the University of Tulsa. As assistant director of the Division of Education Programs at the National Endowment for the Humanities, she directed the three federal programs that supported undergraduate education in the humanities. She also has served as chair of the English Department at Ithaca College, as visiting associate professor at Princeton University, as president of the Boca Raton Community Hospital Foundation and vice president for the Hospital, and for several years as a senior consultant for Academic Search.

Dr. Pierce is the recipient of the Council for Advancement and Support of Education (CASE) District VIII Distinguished Leadership Award for 2003. She has served on the boards of the Association of American Colleges and Universities (AAC&U) and the American Conference of Academic Deans, on the Executive Committee of the Annapolis Group, on the advisory committee for the AAC&U project on engineering and the liberal arts, on the Council of Presidents of the Association of Governing Boards, and on the Washington Women in Leadership Advisory Committee. She has been active in many civic, cultural, and professional organizations, cofounded the University of Puget Sound Access to College program in collaboration with the Tacoma Public Schools, and served from 1998 to 2002 on the National Institute of Alcohol Abuse and Alcoholism Task Force on College Drinking.

Susan Pierce received her bachelor's degree from Wellesley College in 1965, her MA degree in English from the University of Chicago in 1966, and her PhD in English from the University of Wisconsin in 1972.

1

Shared Governance: Its History and Its Challenges

Tensions over governance have been part of the fabric of American college and university life since the latter part of the 1800s. Concerns about academic freedom were initially at the heart of these tensions, but over time, especially since the mid-1960s, conflicts about governance have been prompted by disagreements between some members of the faculty and the administration and sometimes the governing board about who should have responsibility for and authority over—or who at least should be consulted about—which decisions.

In 1966, the American Association of University Professors (AAUP), in collaboration with the American Council on Education (ACE) and the Association of Governing Boards (AGB), defined the notion of shared governance more fully than had been done in the past. As I will discuss more fully later in this chapter, the AAUP argued that even as the governing board had ultimate authority for the institution, the board should delegate the college or university's operations to the president, who in turn would delegate to the faculty primary responsibility for academic matters. This notion was accepted by a great many colleges and universities in concept, despite variations in how it was carried out in practice.

I believe that something even more serious than the historical tensions about governance is now occurring. Specifically, I am convinced that the notion of shared governance as it has been generally understood and at least loosely practiced since 1966 is now being shattered on many campuses and is in jeopardy on other campuses.

Significant economic and political pressures have, on the one hand, led many boards to call for immediate campus responses to problems. It is no longer acceptable to many trustees that, as the old saw goes, it is easier to move a graveyard than to change the curriculum. Some of them judge the traditions of shared governance to be unnecessarily process-laden and time-consuming. Some believe that the very notion of shared governance is no longer viable.

Many presidents share that same sense of urgency and so are making decisions, including those that affect the academic programs, more quickly than was traditionally the case. Sometimes, presidents do so without full or even any consultation with the faculty. In response, those faculty members who believe that they no longer have a say in academic matters, matters of institutional significance, or both are apt publicly to protest presidential and even board decisions. In what appear to be increasing numbers, members of the faculty are going so far as to vote that they have no confidence in their president.

Such adversarial relationships are occurring at a time when our colleges and universities need not conflict but the shared wisdom and perspectives of all constituents. Failures of collaboration among the faculty, the president, and the board, whatever the cause, are inevitably destructive (as they are in all organizations). At the least, failures of collaboration can lead to an unhealthy paralysis in which decisions are delayed or not made at all. At the worst, such failures can throw an institution into crisis.

In addition, conflicts over governance sometimes lead some of the players—faculty, presidents, and trustees—to say and do things that are not in the best interests of themselves or of their institutions. For example, on a campus filled with tension between the president and the faculty, a longtime trustee known for his candor told concerned faculty members—all of whom had tenure—in a public meeting that if they were unhappy with the president's decisions, they should resign and go find another job. The faculty in attendance concluded that the trustees did not understand or value their work. Some worried that the comment meant that the trustees wanted to get rid of tenure. There was a good deal of conversation in the hallways of the college about the value of tenure in protecting free speech.

Several faculty members responded unprofessionally. They told the story to their students, thereby eliciting their support. Some of the students then held a rally to call for the president's resignation and to denounce the board. They invited the local press, who covered the rally in a series about what it called a crisis on campus. Rumors spread that some faculty members were encouraging enrolled students to transfer.

Although the trustees understood that only a few members of the faculty members had involved the students, they were critical of the faculty as a whole, arguing that responsible faculty members should have stood up to and opposed those who had involved the students.

The board remained unified in its support of the president. The faculty became increasingly alienated. Admissions and retention did suffer.

The Pressures on Shared Governance

In my judgment, there are a number of particular catalysts for the movement away from shared governance, including the following:

- As noted earlier, the extremely daunting economic pressures facing most institutions have led some presidents and also some chief academic officers to make unilateral decisions about academic programs, decisions that traditionally had relied on at least the advice if not the consent of the faculty.

- The growing concern, on the part of faculty members at institutions of all sizes and types, that a "corporate" approach to decision making has replaced a more collaborative approach and has led many faculty members vigorously to defend faculty prerogatives because they believe these prerogatives protect them from capricious decisions on the part of administrators and, in some cases, trustees.

• The nature of the professoriate has changed dramatically, in that currently only 25 percent of the faculty at US colleges and universities are tenured or on the tenure-track, with the result that 75 percent of college and university faculty today are contingent faculty, hired on a contract basis, with no role in governance. More than 80 percent of them are part-time. As a result, the vast majority of faculty typically play no role whatsoever in governance.

• The rapid pace of change in the society at large is putting pressure on colleges and universities to institute rapid change as well.

• The growing skepticism among elected officials about the value of higher education has led some governors and some boards of public universities to influence or seek to influence matters that previously had been the province of the administration and sometimes the faculty.

• Some trustees, presidents, and elected officials have embraced the theory advanced by Clayton M. Christensen and Henry J. Eyring in their 2011 Jossey-Bass book, *The Innovative University: Changing the DNA of Higher Education from the Inside Out*, that the traditional model of higher education is no longer sustainable. In particular, they have accepted Christensen and Eyring's view that such disruptive technologies as online education, including MOOCs (massive open online courses), will be more cost-effective and efficient than conventional classrooms. They also subscribe to Christensen and Eyring's view that aspiring colleges and universities need to innovate rather than to imitate—that is, that they need to abandon the habit of emulating the most prestigious institutions like Harvard in order to achieve a higher place in the college rankings and to climb the "Carnegie ladder," the categories developed by the Carnegie Foundation for the Advancement of Teaching.

- Faculty members, in contrast, are often skeptical about whether online learning, especially when it is not supplemented by direct interaction with a professor, is pedagogically effective and of a high quality. Faculty members are particularly skeptical about the MOOCs, which are created by for-profit organizations.

- Fewer chief academic officers than in the past are seeking presidencies and so, for that reason as well as others, boards are increasingly turning to so-called "nontraditional candidates" for the presidency—that is, persons from outside the academy.

- The power, reach, and ease of social media, as is true in other sectors and as later chapters will illustrate, have transformed conflicts that previously would have been confined to a campus and perhaps its local community into matters that quickly receive national and even international attention. Such attention in turn often exacerbates the original conflicts. For example, social media campaigns mounted by faculty and students to broadcast their concerns beyond the campus often motivate geographically distant alumni to become involved in conflicts at their alma mater and the local and national press to weigh in on the issues. National attention has also increasingly motivated governors and other public officials to become actors in dramas affecting state-supported institutions.

Differences in How Shared Governance Has Been Practiced

A great many colleges and universities have embraced and continue at least to give lip service to the notion of shared governance in its broadest outlines.

At most colleges and universities, the board has historically delegated authority to the president for finances, facilities, human resources, risk management, informational technology, fundraising, marketing, external relations, student life, admissions, and financial aid, reserving for itself both oversight of the president and responsibility for policy. The board has also had responsibility for determining the institution's mission, although changes to mission happen only rarely if at all and usually are based on a presidential recommendation developed only after extensive discussions with all campus constituencies and sometimes alumni.

The president in turn has typically delegated responsibility to the faculty, except in unusual circumstances, for all academic matters. What this delegation means on any particular campus tends to grow out of campus history, culture, and governing documents. For example, at some institutions, the faculty's role, even in terms of academic matters, has clearly been understood to be only a recommending one. At yet other institutions, however, the faculty's role in shared governance has extended beyond the academic programs and the hiring, tenure, and promotion of faculty into many other areas of the institution, such as policies and practices relating to students, the cocurriculum, athletics, admissions, financial aid, facilities, and investment of the endowment.

But wherever an institution falls on this spectrum, all decisions that involve the allocation of resources require administrative approval. Thus, initiatives developed and approved by the faculty for academic programs and for faculty lines (including their location) are dependent on the concurrence of the administration (often the president or the chief academic officer) and the allocation of pertinent resources.

The History of Shared Governance

Governance was not an issue on US college campuses prior to the Civil War because, as W. P. Metzger notes in his oft-cited 1955 Columbia University book, *Academic Freedom in the Age of the University*, antebellum colleges were "paternalistic and authoritarian" (p. 5). Explaining that colleges were under "denominational control," Metzger characterized them as looking "to antiquity for the tools of thought, to Christianity for the by-laws of living; [they] supplied furniture and discipline for the mind, but constrained intellectual adventure . . ." (p. 4).

In his essay "Professionalism as the Basis for Academic Freedom and Faculty Governance," Larry Gerber (2010) writes that "before the last quarter of the nineteenth century, college teaching was not a very prestigious vocation" and that, prior to the Civil War, faculty were "aspiring young clergymen who saw college teaching as a temporary position until they could find a pulpit" and who played no role in governance. Rather, Gerber writes:

> Presidents and governing boards, which before the mid-nineteenth century drew heavily from the clergy, exercised decision-making authority with little input from faculty. Faculty were responsible for maintaining discipline, building character, and passing on received wisdom to their students, but were not expected to engage in research or the production of new knowledge (p. 5).

The Emergence of Academic Freedom and Research

After the Civil War, many American professors studied in Germany and, as Gerber notes, soon embraced the German notions that students had the freedom to learn without much administrative interference and that faculty members were free to teach and engage in research as they saw fit. Many American professors also emulated German scholars by valuing research intended to discover new knowledge. Some came to believe that it was important to use that new knowledge to inform public policy debates about economic and social issues. It was no longer thought to be enough for faculty merely to transmit what they knew to their students.

Not unexpectedly, when faculty participated in public policy debates, some found themselves in conflict with corporate donors who on occasion demanded their dismissal. Sometimes these donors were successful. For example, such noted social scientists as Edward A. Bemis, John R. Commons, and Edward A. Ross all lost their academic positions at Chicago, Syracuse, and Stanford, respectively, reportedly because their publicly stated views antagonized donors. Indeed, Mrs. Leland Stanford was the force behind Ross's firing.

The desire for academic freedom and the ability to participate in public policy debates in the public arena was gathering support at the same time that the governance of colleges and universities was also changing in an important way. Increasingly, boards of colleges and universities, whose role was to provide oversight and to hire and if necessary fire the president, included more businessmen and bankers than clergy.

As a result, as Margesson notes, as early as 1908, there were complaints that colleges and universities had become too corporate and that presidents had too much power, something that nearly a century later is very much a refrain on some campuses. A piece about university administrators in the 1908 *Popular Mechanics Monthly* put it this way:

> No single thing has done more harm to higher education in America during the past quarter-century than the steady aggrandizement of the presidential offices and the modeling of university administration upon the methods and ideals of the factory or department store (Margesson, 2008, p. 72).

The AAUP Becomes a Force in Matters of Governance

In 1914, in response to a number of cases during the previous decades in which faculty members believed that academic freedom had been violated, a group of notable scholars came together to form the AAUP.

They founders of the AAUP, including its first president, John Dewey, were particularly influenced by the Ross case and the case of Scott Nearing, whose contract in 1915 had not been renewed at the University of Pennsylvania's Wharton School despite his having been recommended by the faculty. As an article in the Spring 2007 *Wharton Alumni Magazine*, "A Radical Who Laid the Groundwork for the Tenure System," explains, Nearing had run afoul of a number of Wharton trustees because of his publicly expressed views opposing child labor and his general progressive views. Nearing, in fact, according to Bertell Ollman in his undated work published by New York University's educational project, *The Ideal of Academic Freedom as the Ideology of Academic Repression, American Style*, emphasized that he opposed child labor in coal mines, despite the fact that an influential Wharton trustee was a mine owner.

The AAUP formed a committee to investigate the case. Its report was highly critical of Penn's actions. Nearing became such a *cause célèbre* that Penn altered its procedures for terminating a faculty member to conform to the AAUP's recommendations. Nearing then went to the University of Toledo, where he was fired in 1917 for opposing the United States' participation in World War II.

1915 Declaration of Principles on Academic Freedom and Academic Tenure

With the primary goal of protecting academic freedom and the Nearing case very much on its mind, the AAUP issued what was the first of many statements of principles, the *1915 Declaration of*

Principles on Academic Freedom and Academic Tenure. This document also was the first to create the notion that boards, the president, and the faculty share in the governance of colleges and universities with "equal responsibilities" except in scientific and educational matters, where the faculty has primary responsibility.

In the *1915 Declaration*, the AAUP defined what it saw as the three critical elements of academic freedom: "freedom of inquiry and research; freedom of teaching within the university or college; and freedom of extramural utterance and action." The *1915 Declaration* also made a distinction between proprietary schools, which exist to fulfill a charge established by donors, and the vast majority of colleges and universities in the country, which the AAUP characterized as a "public trust."

The *1915 Declaration* further argued that even though faculty members are appointed by the institution's board, they are not employees. Rather, they have a primary responsibility to the public and "to the judgment of [their] profession." Perhaps even more critically, the *1915 Declaration* asserted that trustees "have neither competency nor moral right to intervene" in the professional activities of the faculty.

One of the most critical statements in terms of governance in the *1915 Declaration* was this: "Official action relating to reappointments and refusals of reappointment should be taken only with the advice and consent of some board or committee representative of the faculty."

Since 1915, the AAUP, in partnership with other higher education organizations, has twice issued revised statements about governance, in part prompted by the climate at the time relating to academic freedom.

1940 Statement of Principles on Academic Freedom and Tenure

The *1940 Statement of Principles on Academic Freedom and Tenure*, a joint effort between the AAUP and the AAC (now the American Association of Colleges and Universities, or the AAC&U),

essentially reaffirms the basic tenets of the *1915 Declaration*. However, the context of the *1940 Statement*—a time when there was widespread discussion about whether the United States should enter World War II—may well explain the additional principles that cautioned faculty members about what they said both in the classroom and without. For example, the *1940 Statement* cautioned:

> Teachers are entitled to freedom in the classroom in discussing their subject, but they should be careful not to introduce into their teaching controversial matter, which has no relation to their subject.

This document further noted that although faculty members should be afforded the rights of free speech of any citizen, "[a]s scholars and educational officers, they should remember that the public may judge their profession and their institution by their utterances."

Academic Freedom and Tenure in the Quest for National Security

This statement was published in 1956 during the McCarthy era, a time when there was great public concern about the presence of communists on college campuses and little tolerance in some quarters for those who dissented from the government. During the so-called "Red Scare," faculty members and others accused of being communists lost their jobs. Many campuses banned controversial speakers. Many public institutions required faculty members to sign loyalty oaths. I think it safe to say that during this period many institutions neither protected academic freedom nor practiced shared governance.

Margesson reports that in that setting, the AAUP took a strong stance in favor of academic freedom, arguing that individuals not be prohibited from teaching positions because of "their beliefs or associations." Without naming communism, the AAUP's statement asserted, "We cannot accept an educational system that is subject to the irresponsible push and pull of contemporary issues" (Margesson, 2008, p. 119). The document also rejected the notion of loyalty oaths. The AAUP took a fair amount of criticism for this report.

1966 Statement on Governance of Colleges and Universities

The pendulum swung back in the 1960s, when faculty and students alike began to question the nature of authority and responsibility. At the same time, as the *1966 Statement* asserted:

> The academic institution, public or private, often has become less autonomous; buildings, research, and student tuition are supported by funds over which the college or university exercises a diminishing control. Legislative and executive governmental authorities, at all levels, play a part in the making of important decisions in academic policy. If these voices and forces are to be successfully heard and integrated, the academic institution must be in a position to meet them with its own generally unified view.

It was in this setting that the AAUP, in collaboration with ACE and AGB, developed the *1966 Statement on Governance of Colleges and Universities*, which more fully defined the notion of shared governance. Although the AAUP does not keep track of how many colleges and universities have formally endorsed this statement by referencing it in their governing documents, the *1966 Statement* is often cited by members of the faculty in cases of disagreement about governance. Moreover, faculty members who believe that the tenets of this statement have been violated can also ask the AAUP to send a team to investigate. If the team discovers sufficient violations, it may recommend censure, and the designated AAUP committee will vote to put the institution on its censure list.

The *1966 Statement* is the most explicit about shared governance, advocating that colleges and universities practice it in the areas of planning, communications, facilities, the budget, and hiring a new president. In brief, the *1966 Statement* explains that even as ultimate authority and responsibility for an institution resides with the governing board, the board typically delegates operational responsibility to the president, while the faculty has primary responsibility for academic programs and educational policy. The *1966 Statement* also asserts that the president's authority is delegated to him or her by both the board and the faculty. In my experience, few if any boards or for that matter presidents would accept the notion that the faculty delegates to the president, and not the other way around. Boards and presidents would also view the faculty's role in most matters other than the curriculum and academic standards as advisory.

In a 2007 piece for the American Association of Colleges and Universities' *Liberal Education*, "What If the Faculty Really Do Assume Responsibility for the Academic Program?," Jerry Gaff summarizes the key tenets of the *1966 Statement*:

> The faculty has *primary* authority over the academic area, including such matters as the curriculum, standards of faculty competence, and standards of student achievement. In this area, the governing board and administration should "concur with the faculty judgment except in rare instances and for compelling reasons which should be stated in detail." The board and administration, the statement says, should have primary authority over mission, strategic direction, physical plant, and fiscal resources. In these areas, the faculty has *secondary* authority and should be consulted and informed about major decisions.

Differences over the Nature and Pace of Change

Many of the conflicts about governance in recent years have been prompted by differing views about who is responsible for the nature and pace of change, particularly but not exclusively when it comes to academic matters. In fact, *Inside Higher Ed,* the *Chronicle of Higher Education,* the *New York Times,* and other national publications now routinely report instances where differences about this question have led to significant schisms among the governing board, the administration, faculty, the staff, the students, and even the alumni.

In today's environment, in which many colleges and universities are struggling to balance their budgets, to deal with declining enrollments and rising tuition discounts, and to determine how to deal with new populations of students and new methods of delivering education, boards and presidents increasingly want to make programmatic decisions, including those in the academic realm, very quickly. They typically also argue that it is essential that their institution be disciplined in how it allocates resources and that it become more entrepreneurial in generating new revenue streams. In contrast, members of the faculty typically resist what they view as hasty decisions and resist even more the involvement of boards and presidents in academic matters. As I will discuss in more detail in later chapters, on many campuses the faculty is losing this battle, with boards and presidents creating structures, policies, and hiring practices that diminish the faculty's role in governance.

The Effect of Program Prioritization on Governance

In light of economic pressures, some presidents, sometimes at the prompting of their trustees, have in recent years initiated efforts to prioritize programs. Often inspired by Robert C. Dickeson's 2010 revision of his Jossey-Bass book, *Prioritizing Academic Programs and Services: Reallocating Resources to Achieve Strategic Balance,* those involved call for a reallocation of resources to programs that advance the institution's mission and to programs "that they can accomplish with distinction" (p. 15).

But Dickeson himself believes that program prioritization almost always elicits resistance from the faculty because, in his view, it "violates the egalitarian ideology in higher education," which Dickeson describes as follows:

> If all programs are more or less equal, who's to judge their relative worth? I'm an expert in one discipline, and I rely on my college experts in other disciplines to do their work. I am just as incapable of judging the value of their work or the worth of their programs as they obviously are of judging mine.

A less generous view of objections to program prioritization is that faculty members have at least a tacit agreement that they will not be critical of or take an adversarial action against another program so long as their colleagues in those programs don't criticize or make such judgments about their programs. It is also the case that the very language of program prioritization concerns faculty, because this language suggests that some programs may no longer be considered a priority and therefore de facto become second-class.

Dickeson also argues that the faculty's "common mistrust of administrators to do anything right unites [the faculty] in opposition to management efforts to poke around in, and likely destroy, what we've worked so hard to establish" (p. 21).

But despite the reluctance of many faculty to participate in the process of evaluating and even making recommendations about the fate of academic programs, increasing numbers of colleges and universities—public and private alike—are discontinuing programs for which there is no longer demand or which for varying reasons are no longer an institutional priority. Those that rely on pre-professional and technical programs are adding and subtracting programs explicitly based on market demands. Some institutions are becoming more experimental and innovative in shifting resources from these programs to new programs that they believe will increase net tuition revenue.

The Creation of Alternative Structures to Skirt Issues of Governance

Until the past decade, few colleges and universities even contemplated offering new academic programs without the engagement and even commitment of the faculty, who for their part, on the one hand, are not susceptible to notions of urgency and, on the other hand, are risk-averse. That practice has changed. Numerous institutions, for instance, that previously had emphasized undergraduate education are now investing in new graduate programs, often in education, the health sciences, and business. Some of these offerings are online. Some take a blended approach, combining on-campus classes with online components. Some take place on satellite campuses. Many rely on part-time adjuncts hired on a contract basis without benefits and who, as chapter 3 explains, have no role in governance.

Despite the fact that some of these new programs are generating significant revenues and subsidizing the undergraduate programs, on some campuses the undergraduate faculty have balked at the reallocation of resources to these new programs. Faculty often argue that these new programs are of a lesser quality or are not tied to the institution's original mission. If these programs are successful, these concerns tend to be ignored because the programs often are keeping the institution afloat.

When confronted with such resistance, a number of presidents have simply created alternative structures for the new programs and new methods of review and approval for these programs. In several instances, presidents simply have created a new graduate school, a school of professional studies, or a school in one of the new disciplines. The deans of these new schools are given the responsibility for and authority over the new programs, including curriculum, hiring, and academic standards.

As I will discuss at some length in chapter 3, the faculty in these programs often are contingent faculty—that is, faculty who are neither tenured nor on the tenure-track and who generally are part-time adjuncts who in fact do not participate in governance at all. In addition, many such new programs are taught online, again by contingent faculty who often are part-time and who also do not typically participate in institutional governance.

Impact of Conflicts over Governance on the Presidency

The contentious environment on many campuses may well be discouraging talented people from considering both the presidency and trusteeship. This is a significant problem because colleges and universities today need presidents and trustees who are intelligent, perceptive, informed, and committed. Colleges and universities also need presidents and trustees who take seriously the fact that they are entrusted with the health and integrity of the colleges and universities they serve.

Just as important, in my judgment, our institutions of higher education need presidents and trustees who understand that the faculty ultimately is the heart and soul of the institution, that an institution's academic mission should drive resource and policy decisions, that ensuring academic quality is paramount, and that protecting academic freedom is essential.

To be successful, in my judgment, presidents need to be able to inspire their faculty colleagues about the president's vision and to lead colleagues at least to understand, if not to agree with, the decisions that the president is making. Presidents need to explain why shared governance, to work, now needs to move much more quickly than in the past. The good news, as the final chapter will illustrate, is that there are such presidents who have led their institutions to change and that there are faculty members and trustees on these campuses who support these presidents' efforts.

I have been struck, nevertheless, in the past several years by how many successful presidents have shared privately with me their concern that the job of being a college president is becoming untenable. These include a handful of presidents, several within their first few years, who have received high praise for being present on their campuses and for spending time actively listening to students, faculty, and staff. Each of them has been an exceptionally good fundraiser.

All of them described their biggest discouragement as being tensions with or even overt conflicts with the faculty, tensions and conflicts that stem from problems not of the president's making. All insisted that although needing to work seven days and evenings a week takes its toll, they had anticipated and acclimated to that. Rather, they described how discouraged they felt when, despite evidence to the contrary, faculty members seemed to assume that they were the enemy.

These presidents were also discouraged by the fact that even actions that they had taken to support the faculty were being criticized. For example, although each of these presidents, despite inheriting budgetary problems, had balanced the budget and given raises of varying percentages to faculty and staff members who had not received raises under the previous administration, each was criticized because the raises were not in the minds of the recipients adequate enough to compensate for the years without raises. One discouraged president described the situation this way: "We worked very hard to give everyone a 2.5 percent raise at the end of my first year even though I had inherited a deficit budget. Rather than being glad, many people told me that they were insulted by the low amount."

Chief Academic Officers Are Increasingly Uninterested in the Presidency

Chief academic officers (CAOs)—provosts, academic vice presidents, and deans—of course witness the dynamic between the president and the faculty, with the result that many of them decide that they do not want to become presidents. The data are clear: declining numbers of CAOs are interested in the presidency.

According to a 2009 ACE report on the college presidency, *National Census of Chief Academic Officers*, more than two-thirds of CAOs do not "intend to seek a presidency, despite ACE data that show the most common path to the president's office is through the chief academic officer." Indeed, that same study shows that currently only 20 percent of CAOs actually go on to become presidents.

The ACE study reports that the major hesitations that CAOs have about becoming presidents are that they "find the nature of presidential work unappealing (66 percent), are ready to retire (32 percent), are concerned about the time demands of the position (27 percent) and don't want to live in a fishbowl (24 percent)."

At the same time, many boards of trustees today believe that their institutions would be best served by a president from outside the academy who, they argue, will bring a fresh perspective to the work of the president and who will have expertise in allocating and reallocating resources and generally in dealing with financial matters.

The implications of the declining interest of CAOs in the presidency and the growing interest on the part of boards to go outside the academy is that increasingly boards are appointing nontraditional candidates as presidents. For instance, ACE reported in *The American College President—2012* that for one out of five presidents, the most recent prior position was outside the academy, "up sharply from 13 percent in 2006 and 15 percent in 2001."

Traditional Versus Nontraditional Presidents

There are certainly examples of very effective nontraditional presidents—that is, those whose professional experience has been outside the academy. University of Oklahoma president David Boren and former Davidson College president Bobby Vagt come immediately to mind. Boren of course was a Rhodes Scholar and then a very effective US senator, and Vagt was a Davidson graduate who throughout a distinguished career remained committed to the college, receiving its Alumni Service Award and serving for two years as national leader of its annual fund and as a member of its board of visitors. His wife and older daughter were Davidson graduates, and his youngest daughter was enrolled as a first-year student.

Although there are certainly many examples of presidents who have come up through the faculty ranks and who have not been successful in their presidential role, in my experience, presidents who have been faculty members have one important advantage over those who come from outside the academic community or who come to their presidency from a vice presidency in a nonacademic area, such as finance, advancement, enrollment, or student affairs. Specifically, people who have themselves been faculty members generally tend to be pretty tolerant of faculty dissension. They are inclined to understand that most people who choose to go into college teaching do so because they are independent, critical thinkers who are used to being given deference for their independent and critical thoughts. Certainly, during my own presidency, I was aware that even though I celebrated the critical stance of my colleagues in terms of their teaching and scholarship, I often wished they would not apply that same approach to what often appeared to me to be everything that I did.

The Difficulties of Dissent for Some Nontraditional Presidents

Dissent about and even overt resistance to presidential decisions on the part of the faculty and sometimes the students can prove very difficult for some nontraditional presidents, particularly those who come from worlds where there is a formal chain of command. The following examples illustrate the difficulty presidents have when they don't fully understand how to manage in an academic environment.

- A new president—used to being a high-level executive in a Fortune 500 company—took any questions about her decisions to be challenges to her personal authority. In fact, she viewed any criticism from members of the faculty as insubordination. As time wore on, she chose to deal with the situation by communicating very little with the faculty, including attending faculty meetings only sporadically. The more she shut down, the more the faculty raised questions. When the faculty senate invited her to attend a meeting of the entire faculty to discuss concerns about a personnel decision that she had made, she refused the invitation, saying that she was doing so on the advice of counsel. The faculty as a whole voted no confidence within months. Her board was confused because her predecessor and faculty members had enjoyed a positive relationship. This president eventually resigned.

- A second nontraditional candidate similarly came to his presidency from the executive suite of a major corporation. Faced with a budget deficit nearly double what he had anticipated, he decided to make cuts. In order to curry favor with the faculty, he decided to leave the faculty and the academic programs intact. He hired an outplacement firm with which he had worked in his corporate role to advise him and then took their advice. The result: on a given day just before the Christmas break, the vice presidents went to the offices of those staff members being terminated, asked them to gather their personal belongings and come with them to a large meeting room on the edge of the campus.

Once the selected staff members were gathered, the vice president for finance explained to them that they were being terminated for budgetary reasons, that each would receive two weeks of severance and that they could come back that evening to the university where, accompanied by campus security, they could clean out their offices. The president, on the advice of the firm, was off campus.

Those who had been terminated included many long-time and admired staff members who provided support to the faculty and who were part of student affairs. The faculty and staff erupted with anger at how their colleagues had been treated. The students created a YouTube video that went viral among the alumni, protesting the decisions and chanting a variation of "Rehire Them!"

This decision continued to haunt the president throughout his presidency. He nevertheless learned that he needed to consult with people on the faculty and staff whom he respected before making major decisions, and over time he and the campus reached a rapprochement of sorts.

• Another nontraditional candidate was named president of the large public university where he had earned a master's degree. As soon as his appointment was announced, he made it known that he wished to be given tenure, something he thought would give him standing with the faculty. The board said that it would consider doing so but that the president had to go through the same sort of review as any new professor. The department met and voted overwhelmingly not to recommend him for tenure, saying that in fact they wouldn't have hired him as a faculty member at all. This was an embarrassment for the new president and an unhappy beginning to his relationship with his new colleagues.

• The nontraditional president of a private college created a crisis with the faculty when he unilaterally announced new criteria for hiring, tenure, and promotions. In preparation for the decision, he had consulted widely with presidents of aspirant institutions, something he shared with his faculty when he announced the changes. The faculty were not impressed. It was they, they explained to him, whom he should have consulted. The board was supportive of the proposed changes and contemplated putting a hold on all tenure decisions unless the faculty approved the president's criteria. This conflict took precedence over all other institutional matters, including the revised core curriculum for which the president had also asked.

Some Talented People Are Reluctant to Serve as Trustees

It should also be of concern that it is not only potential presidents who now may have hesitations about service. The negative attention that has recently focused on such boards as those at the University of Virginia and Penn State may well lead some potentially talented trustees to be reluctant to serve as board members. Moreover, growing expectations for trustee donations may discourage some capable people from board service.

Pressures on Trustees, Presidents, and Faculty to Change

No alternative model to the traditional notions of shared governance has yet to emerge. Even so, the pressures facing colleges and universities today clearly demand that trustees, presidents (and other senior administrators), and faculty members redefine their roles and responsibilities and work collaboratively in new and more effective ways. Fortunately there are many healthy and thriving institutions where the president, the faculty, and the board work together effectively.

In these institutions, the president welcomes and in fact actively seeks the participation of the faculty in decision making about academic matters. She or he understands and actively considers the perspective of the faculty. In these institutions, because faculty members have confidence in the president and the senior administration, they devote most of their time, attention, energy, and intellectual power to teaching, advising, and scholarship. Faculty members also generously engage in service because they believe that this work is meaningful, will contribute to the education of their students, and will advance the institution's academic mission. In these institutions, with the president's encouragement and help, the trustees understand and value the work of the faculty, and the faculty appreciates rather than demonizes the board.

The strains that I have described in this chapter are both the result of and exacerbated by the various economic pressures that colleges and universities have experienced in the last decade, including but not exclusively those caused by the economic downturn of 2008. The next chapter will also describe the ways in which these economic pressures have impacted institutional functioning, priorities, and governance.

2

The Impact of Financial Pressures on Governance

Today, many colleges and universities find themselves with structural deficits that have an impact on their ability to thrive and in some instances even to survive. Although there have always been institutions that at various points in their history have suffered from constrained resources, what is different today, according to Moody's, is that most of the sector is in financial jeopardy. For example, in January 2012, Moody's gave a stable outlook only to the "diversified market-leading colleges and universities with strong market positions and balance sheets and multiple revenue-generating business lines." Perhaps even more important, Moody's has given a negative outlook "for the bulk of rated colleges and universities, which are far more dependent on state appropriations, student tuition, or both."

In addition, because the structural deficits on many campuses have eluded easy solutions, presidents and their chief financial officers are now focusing on both the cost and the revenue sides of the academic programs, areas that previously had been "off limits" at most institutions. As chapter 5 will discuss in some detail, this focus on the academic programs often strains the relationship between the faculty and the administration and sometimes between the faculty and the board.

The Causes of Financial Pressures

Financial deficits on campuses often stem from declining enroll-ments, increases in the percentage of tuition dollars that are dedicated to financial aid in an effort to enroll and retain the desired number of students, shortfalls in anticipated gifts, decreases in the size of the endowment, smaller than anticipated income from the endowment, or some combination of these. The 2008 economic downturn magnified these problems. So did the fact that so many institutions in the past decade borrowed heavily, often incurring significantly greater debt service than they had in the past.

The Impact of the 2008 Economic Downturn

Beginning in 2008, students and their families became more concerned than ever with cost and value and so have increasingly become less willing to commit the resources they once had to a college education. As Sallie Mae points out in its report *How America Pays for College 2012: National Study of College Students and Parents*, parents in 2011–12 reduced their contribution for their children's college education by 11 percent from the previous year and by 32 percent from the year before that.

This significant decline in parental support for higher educa-tion has meant that many campuses now are not achieving their budgeted number for enrollment. Because most colleges and uni-versities are dependent on tuition, such enrollment shortfalls often throw them into deficits. Moreover, any shortfall in first-year enroll-ments will be felt in terms of revenue (in many instances, room and board as well as tuition) for at least four years, and any shortfall in transfers will be felt for at least one to three years.

Some of the pertinent statistics are these:

• Although overall college enrollments declined only modestly in 2010–11, many individual campuses suffered drops, with Moody's reporting that 41 percent of private colleges and universities suffered declining enrollments. The National Association of College and University Business Officers (NACUBO) reported in its *2011 Tuition Discounting Study* that more than one-third of these institutions suffered declines of at least 5 percent.

- In its *2012 Tuition Discounting Study*, NACUBO reported that enrollment declines continued in 2011–12. For example, total undergraduate enrollments were down at 45.6 percent of participating institutions from the year before. NACUBO presented an especially dire picture in 2011–12 for a subset of institutions—that is, private colleges with enrollments of fewer than 4,000 students. Specifically, a stunning 83 percent of such colleges suffered an enrollment decline.

- Many colleges and universities, concerned about enrollment, increased the use of institutional grant dollars for financial aid. For example, in 2011–12, private colleges discounted tuition by 45 percent, a record high.

- For the 2012–13 academic year, Moody's predicted that revenues would either decline or remain stagnant. According to its Investors Service's fourth annual tuition survey:

> Weakened pricing power and difficulty in growing enrollment are impeding revenue growth at an increasing number of US colleges and universities. Moody's found that a third of private colleges and universities expect net tuition revenue to either decline or grow at a rate below inflation in fiscal year 2013. In all, 17% of both private and public universities are expecting declines in net tuition revenue, while another 16% are expecting percent increases that are less than the rate of inflation.

In this same report, Moody's analyst Emily Schwarz noted that both uncertain job prospects and "tougher governmental scrutiny of higher education costs and disclosure practices [are] adding regulatory and political pressure to prevent tuition and revenue from rising at past rates."

The Consequences of Aggressive Borrowing

A number of colleges and universities, large and small, highly endowed and tuition-dependent, have in recent years found themselves saddled with excessive debt service, raising questions about the judgment of some presidents and, as critically, the adequacy of board oversight. Indeed, among the board's top fiduciary responsibilities is to seek to ensure the financial health of the institution. Providing guidance to and oversight of the administration in terms of investing the endowment and borrowing is central to this responsibility.

The first decade of this century was one of a great deal of borrowing, often to build new facilities and renovate existing ones as part of a college or university's competitive strategy. Moody's reports that from 2000 to 2011, at the more than 500 colleges and universities that it rates, debt (adjusted for inflation) more than doubled. For example, debt in inflation-adjusted dollars at the Julliard School rose from $6 million to $195 million, at Miami University from $66 million to $326 million, and at New York University from $1.2 billion to $2.8 billion. At Syracuse University, from 2004 to 2013, debt rose from $150 million to $400 million. Although each of these institutions has been able to absorb this debt service, the two examples that follow, schools as disparate as Harvard University and Calvin College, illustrate the negative impact that excessive debt can have on a campus, even one as affluent as Harvard.

In addition, meeting this debt service required many institutions with limited resources to eliminate programs, lay off faculty and staff, cut benefits, freeze salaries, defer maintenance, and make other difficult and often unpopular resource decisions. Often these decisions were made at the administrative level, with little if any faculty involvement, even though some of them clearly affected the nature and quality of the academic programs and the nature of faculty positions.

Harvard University

In June 2008, Harvard's endowment had grown to an unprecedented $36.9 billion. A year later, that number had dropped to $26 billion. The university also around this time over a three-year period doubled its annual debt service from $3 billion to $6 billion. Nina Munk's extended story in the August 2009 *Vanity Fair*, "Rich Harvard, Poor Harvard," about Harvard's significant financial problems sent shock waves through the higher education community, given the abundance of Harvard's resources. If, the narrative went, Harvard was facing serious financial problems, what did that mean for the vast majority of colleges and universities that had paltry endowments and were tuition-dependent?

Munk reports that there was a good deal of finger-pointing about who was responsible for these financial problems, with some blaming the decision of members of the Harvard Management Company to leave the university and go out on their own in the face of complaints about the compensation of some investors, working on commission. For example, Jon Jacobson, in 1995 made $6 million or, as Munk put it, approximately 25 times more than Harvard's president, Neil Rudenstein. The following year, Jacobson earned $7.6 million and, in 1998, $10.2 million. Others attributed the problems to then president Larry Summers and Robert Rubin, a member of the Harvard Corporation or its governing board, for "meddling" with Jack Meyer, who ran the Management Company until he left in 2005. In other words, there was at the very least ambiguity about who had oversight over Harvard's investments: its president, an individual member of the Corporation, or the Corporation as a whole.

After 2008, Harvard responded to these budgetary woes by making significant cuts in its operating budgets, laying off hundreds of workers and suspending work on its ambitious Allston project, which it had intended to finance with a combination of debt and gifts. The university also increased class size, deferred maintenance, stopped serving hot breakfasts to undergraduates in its residential houses, and downgraded junior-varsity sports to club sports. The university also took steps to make operations more efficient. Even so, in FY 2011, Harvard had a $130 million deficit on a $3.9 billion operating budget.

Harvard has now made it clear that all future capital projects will require substantial fundraising and will not rely on debt. For example, the university has decided to go forward with a much scaled-down Allston project, to be funded with gifts rather than borrowing.

Calvin College

In February 2013, Calvin College's relatively new president, Michael Le Roy, announced that the college had accrued $115 million in debt with an endowment of $442 million. There were two deliberate choices that the college had made that led to this debt. In both cases, the trustees had approved of the actions. First, the college had been dedicating only 0.9 percent of its annual operating budget to debt service even though the debt service comprised 6 percent of the college's expenses. Second, the college had decided to invest funds from gifts for capital projects and instead to fund those projects through borrowing in the belief that income from the invested funds would pay for the debt service. Investments, however, did not yield anywhere near the expected revenue.

Faced with debt service that now required 10 percent of the operating budget, Calvin soon laid off twenty-two staff and faculty members and reduced its contribution to health benefits for current and retired faculty and staff. On the good news side of the ledger, the college reported a $3.4 million increase in gifts over the previous year.

Scott Spoekhof, the chair of the Calvin College Board of Trustees, in a letter to the campus acknowledged that the board had failed to provide adequate oversight and had been acting without full information. Specifically, Spoekhof wrote that through the campus review and assessment prompted by the budget shortfall, the board "identified several things that contributed to the issue, including recognition that stronger board oversight may have detected the issues earlier. . . . Yes, in hindsight the board would have greatly benefited from having the detail of information we have today regarding cost overruns and investment strategies."

Declining State Support for Public Universities

In addition to the pressures facing all colleges and universities, public institutions have been confronted with drastic cuts in state support, which have put often-extreme pressure on their operating budgets. Specifically, Moody's reported in June 2012 that the states are "spending 20 percent less in inflation-adjusted dollars on higher education than a decade ago." A March 6, 2013 press release from the State Higher Education Executive Officers Association (SHEEO) is even more specific: "Per student support in 2012 is $5,896, the lowest level in . . . 25 years," noting "a 9 percent decrease in state and local support per student in constant dollars from 2011." As context, in 2001, state support provided $8,670 in constant dollars per student.

Not unexpectedly, the reduction in state support has led to increases in tuition and fees. As a result, as the SHEEO press release explained, "over the past 25 years, the percentage of educational revenue supported by tuition has climbed steadily from 23.3 percent in 1987 to 47.0 percent in 2012."

At the same time, enrollments at some public universities have actually increased, leading to larger classes. In response to this circumstance, some institutions have capped enrollment. California State University earned headlines in 2012 for announcing that it would give preference to graduate students from outside California because the tuition of out-of-state students is much higher than that of Californians. As Scott Jaschik put it in "Rejected for Being In-State," an August 13, 2012 *Inside Higher Ed* piece, "Given that [in-state] tuition covers only a fraction of the costs of these students' education, the university said it couldn't afford them."

The Impact of Constrained Resources on Salaries

Compensation is the largest line item in the expense budget of most organizations and certainly of most colleges and universities, but until recently many campuses mainly looked elsewhere for cost savings. Instead, they deferred maintenance, reduced travel funds, outsourced operations, and entered into shared purchasing agreements. Some reduced support for professional development for staff and faculty. Others charged for printing. Some campuses eliminated all entertaining and no longer funded the serving of all food at campus meetings.

The one area where many campuses reduced compensation costs was by shifting instructional responsibilities away from tenured and tenure-track faculty to contract or so-called contingent faculty, the majority of whom are part-time adjuncts. Chapter 3 will explore the implications of this trend.

Since 2008, many colleges and universities have begun to make cuts in additional ways that affect both the faculty and the staff, including lay-offs, salary freezes, furloughs, and a reduction in the institution's contribution to benefits, including health and retirement benefits.

The impact of constrained resources on salaries since 2008 has been especially significant. According to the AAUP report on faculty salaries, *No Refuge*, in 2009–10 faculty members received an average raise of 1.2 percent (inflation was 2.7 percent), the lowest increase in salaries in the fifty years that the organization has been surveying salaries. Moreover, at the 1,141 institutions surveyed, two-thirds either cut faculty salaries, gave no raises, or increased salaries on average less than 2 percent. In its 2012 report

A Very Slow Recovery, the AAUP reported that inflation continued to outpace salary increases in that in 2011–12, faculty salaries nationally rose 1.8 percent while inflation was 3 percent.

Although I know of no similar analysis of staff salaries, one can confidently assume that—other than at the presidential level—the status of staff salaries is either similar to that of the faculty or even less promising.

In contrast, presidential salaries have, according to the AAUP, grown at a higher rate than that of faculty members. For example, the AAUP reports:

> Over the four-year period [between 2006–07 and 2010–11] inflation-adjusted median presidential salaries increased by 9.8 percent. By contrast, full-time faculty salaries remained flat at doctoral universities, increased by less than half a percent at baccalaureate and community colleges, and rose by less than 2 percent at master's universities.

This disparity between faculty and presidential salaries often fuels discontent on campuses. And although the vast majority of presidents do not make extravagant salaries, the annual newspaper accounts about those several dozen presidents who are making well over a million dollars a year further fuel that discontent.

Efforts to Control Tuition and Limit Growing Financial Aid

To try to shore up enrollments, many colleges and universities in recent years have increased the share of their operating budget dedicated to financial aid. For example, as noted earlier, in 2011–12, private colleges discounted tuition by 45 percent, a record high. For that same year, as the National Association of Independent Colleges and Universities (NAICU) points out in its study *New Affordability Measures at Private, Nonprofit Colleges and Universities:*

Academic Year 2012–13, a number of institutions, such as Cabrini College, the College of Charleston, Duquesne, Seton Hall, and the University of the South, tried to increase their competitiveness by either stabilizing or reducing their "sticker price," or the published number for tuition, for at least some if not all of their students. Others, like Kettering University and William & Mary, "locked" tuition in for four years for each incoming first-year class.

These trends have continued. For example, for the 2013–14 academic year, NAICU reports that twenty-nine private colleges have frozen tuition, several, like Mt. Holyoke, for the second year in a row. Roger Williams and the Sage Colleges have guaranteed that tuition will not increase for students for a four-year period. A few colleges are giving four-year graduation guarantees, have capped loans, or are reimbursing student loans if the students meet certain criteria.

The Consequences of Increased Financial Aid and Less Tuition

The higher tuition discounts at many institutions and the decision to reduce tuition has in at least some instances resulted in the very thing that these institutions hoped to avoid: reduced net tuition revenue. In fact, despite the fact that, according to the AAUP's *A Very Slow Recovery*, tuition and fees, when adjusted for inflation, have in the last decade increased by 72 percent, net tuition at private colleges and universities has dropped. NAICU's website about college affordability reports: "Average inflation-adjusted net tuition and fees at private colleges has actually dropped by 3.5 percent from 2007–08 to 2012–13."

The implications of reduced net tuition are obvious. As institutions devote an ever-greater share of their budgets to financial aid, they must cut in other areas. In addition to the cuts described earlier, many colleges and universities are now foregoing new technology, increasing class size, and either freezing or reducing departmental operating budgets, all of which have an impact on teaching and learning.

Although typically decisions about tuition and financial aid have been made by the administration, subject to board approval, increasingly members of the faculty are therefore now calling for their participation in such matters. Their argument: such decisions may be central to the institution's mission, will almost certainly affect the way resources are allocated to the academic programs, and are likely to affect the nature and quality of the student body. There are also a number of examples of student and alumni protests over decisions about tuition and financial aid.

Faculty and Students Want More Say in Financial Decisions

Because faculty members have been and will continue to be directly affected by financial decisions, increasing numbers are now seeking a more significant role in terms of their institution's financial policies and the allocation of resources that lie outside the academic programs. In the past, these areas would have been considered to be the province of the administration. For example, protests have erupted over financial aid policy and tuition at Wesleyan University and Cooper Union, respectively. Grinnell offers a counterexample where a transparent and inclusive process, at least for the time being, forestalled conflicts.

Wesleyan Limits Need-Blind Admissions

Faced with escalating financial aid, the Wesleyan University administration, in the fall of 2012, decided that it would end the practice of need-blind admissions for the entire student body and instead would take into account family income and the ability to pay full tuition for what the university expects will be the last 10 percent of each freshmen class that it admits, most typically those admitted from the waiting list. As Kevin Kiley pointed out in his June 1, 2012 *Inside Higher Ed* piece, "Need Too Much," in making this decision, the university argued that a need-blind policy for all students was no longer financially sustainable.

Although Wesleyan had been in a distinct minority of very affluent schools that practiced need-blind admission for all students, the faculty and students at Wesleyan have vigorously and publicly protested this administrative decision. Critics of the decision have formed a "Need-Blind Focus Group" and claim that this change in policy will result in discrimination in the admissions process based on socioeconomic class and that the decision was made without consultation and transparency. The protests have included a banner at graduation, a peaceful sit-in of the president's office, the creation of a student government task force, a confrontation between students and the president, and an alumni website encouraging Wesleyan graduates not to give to the university to protest the decision.

Cooper Union Decides to Charge Tuition

Founded in 1959 by industrialist Peter Cooper, who wanted to give students access to an education of high quality that was "open and free to all," the Cooper Union for the Advancement of Science and Art in New York has never charged tuition. Now faced with a significant deficit, the board voted to begin charging tuition of up to $20,000.

Cooper Union students, faculty, and alumni were joined by students and faculty from other New York City colleges and universities for a day in May protesting the decision. Cooper Union students then held a nine-week sit-in in the office of President Jamshed Bharucha, who inherited a deficit of nearly $17 million when he became president in 2011. Students have also circulated a petition calling for the president's firing. Some of those protesting also blame the board for having made a series of financially costly decisions, including building a new $175 million engineering building.

The students ended the sit-in when they were promised that the institution would revisit the issue and involve students, faculty members, and alumni in a process that originally had been limited to the administration and then board. In addition, in a major change in how the governing board functioned, the students were promised representation on the board of trustees. The agreement reportedly also granted the protesting students amnesty and promised to create a student center.

Grinnell College Affirms Need-Blind Admission for Next Two Years

Grinnell College, too, has taken a hard look at its need-blind approach to admission. President Raynard Kington approached the issue in an intentionally transparent way, sharing with the campus and the public the financial challenges that Grinnell, even with its $1.5 billion endowment, is facing because of its high tuition discount. Without changing its approach to financial aid, Grinnell was facing an increase over the next few years from its already very high 62 percent tuition discount to 70 percent.

After a campuswide study that involved all Grinnell constituencies, the board has agreed to keep Grinnell's need-blind approach for the next two years, at which time it may revisit the question. In the meantime, the college is increasing its merit aid in the hopes of attracting wealthier students, is raising loan limits, and is seeking to identify previously unreported assets for students receiving financial aid, for instance, from noncustodial parents. The campus is pleased about the decision, although some have expressed worries that the effort to attract a greater number of wealthier students may be unfair to those without such means.

Both the process and the decision to continue the current policy at least for two years clearly helped Grinnell avoid the protests that Wesleyan has experienced.

The Dangers of Business as Usual in Times of Budget Problems

Some institutions, even before 2008, had assumed that their financial problems would be of short duration and so hoped simply to ride out whatever storm they were experiencing, assuming mistakenly that in time things would go back to normal. Thus, instead of making decisions to cut expenses or aggressively try to attract new revenues when confronted with budget shortfalls, these colleges and universities continued to budget for the status quo and generally to function as they always had.

Inevitably, these colleges and universities decided that the status quo was not in any way financially sustainable. But because the deficits had accumulated over time, these institutions often found themselves in crisis and needed to take draconian measures to survive. Alice W. Brown, in her 2012 Stylus book, *Cautionary Tales: Strategy Lessons from Struggling Colleges*, makes the point that many of the institutions that closed because of financial reasons were in denial until it became too late.

The Dangers of Ongoing Structural Deficits

In the past several years I learned about an especially vivid example of how a president and a board, by failing to take decisive and responsible action about their institution's structural deficit, can damage their institution for the long term.

This college had throughout its history enjoyed a reputation for offering undergraduates a high-quality liberal arts education. Its long-term president had for more than two decades recommended to the board deficit budgets of $3 million to $5 million for the institution's annual operating budget, and the board had approved those budgets. She had assured her trustees that deficit budgeting was standard practice in higher education.

The campus community was unaware of the deficits. Faculty and staff continued to enjoy standard raises. The college periodically added new programs, occasionally added some new faculty and staff positions, and built a beautiful new academic building. No programs or positions were eliminated. People were concerned about the amount of deferred maintenance, particularly in the residence halls and the student center, but otherwise everything seemed to be fine.

When this president announced her plans to retire, the financial vice president immediately took a job at another institution. Deciding that it wanted the next president to select a new CFO, the board went with an interim vice president from the existing staff. During the search, the board told candidates what it believed to be the case: the college had some financial challenges, but apparently neither they nor the candidate they chose as their next president understood the magnitude of the problem.

The new president quickly recognized that during his predecessor's tenure, the institution had funded more than $70 million of deficits by drawing down the endowment. He brought in a consultant to determine what level of enrollment the institution would need in order to maintain the status quo and was alarmed to learn that it would need to increase enrollment immediately by at least 25 percent. Since the college had also been experiencing declining enrollments, it did not seem feasible that it would be able to increase enrollment that dramatically and that quickly.

The president opened the books to the campus as a way of explaining why the college was going to need to lay off a significant number of staff members, reduce benefits, institute a faculty and staff hiring freeze other than for admissions, freeze salaries, and reduce departmental budgets immediately. He decided at the time not to make cuts in the academic programs, hoping that would earn him faculty support. He also decided that the college needed aggressively to increase enrollment and so put additional funds into financial aid. He asked the faculty to identify new programs that it thought might attract new populations of students.

Unfortunately over the next several years, enrollments remained static. At the same time, the faculty found it hard to imagine how it would create new programs without increasing the size of the faculty and so generated few new ideas.

The initial steps to reduce the deficit by no means eliminated it. The president anticipates a new round of cuts that this time will involve faculty positions and several academic programs. Faculty members, who are unhappy that they have had no salary increases in seven years, are now worried about job security. Members of the staff have the same worries. A number of people have left the institution for other jobs and others are looking. Needless to say, everyone is worried about the future.

When a trustee whom I know and admire, a respected professor of finance at one of the country's most prestigious institutions, shared with me his concerns about the college, I asked him why the board had failed to fulfill its fiduciary responsibility to provide oversight of the former president and to ensure the financial health of the college and why he personally had not objected to these deficit budgets. His response: the board liked and wanted to support the president, and for his part, even though he knew that these growing deficits would over time mean trouble for the institution, he didn't want to appear to be questioning the judgment of the president or of his fellow trustees. He added that the board was giving the new president three more years to resolve the budget problems and so were going to continue to approve deficit budgets for that period.

The faculty has less patience than the board and is now seeking a greater role in governance and in the budget process. For example, a new faculty committee on governance has asked to have faculty representatives serve on all board committees with voice and vote and to have a faculty representative serve on the board with voice but not vote. They have called for a more transparent and participatory budget process. At the same time, many faculty members have become alienated and now refuse to serve on committees, to meet with prospective students, and to speak to alumni groups. Faculty members are also expressing concerns to one another and to some trustees that the college has developed no viable plans to address the deficit.

Wish List Budgets

There is also the phenomenon of presidents who recommend budgets to their boards based on either their hopes and dreams or their perceived needs rather than on realistic projections and whose boards fail to provide appropriate oversight and instead approve those budgets. One such president went so far as to build into the annual operating budget a number for anticipated bequests even though those committing to the bequests were very much alive. He selected the budget number for gifts based on what the institution needed to fill its gap between the university's projected expenses and anticipated revenues. In most years, those who had set up the bequests did not die, and so the bequests did not materialize, resulting in a deficit.

In another such instance, a new president of a university that had enjoyed significant surpluses for decades wanted an infusion of new revenue to fund several new costly initiatives that he favored. He therefore instructed the financial vice president to increase the budgeted numbers for first-year students and transfers. The financial vice president tried to dissuade him but to no avail. The president also recommended to the board that because the institution had little debt, it would be prudent to borrow $100 million to build a new student center and a new athletics complex. The board, lulled by the college's success for decades, approved the budget and the borrowing. The financial vice president resigned to take a position elsewhere.

The following fall, the entering first-year class and transfers not only did not meet the inflated budget numbers, they came in under the historical numbers as well. The institution was now faced with a substantial deficit at the same time that it needed significantly to increase the share of the operating budget that covered debt service.

A number of senior faculty members on this campus have become restive, worried that the campus has gone so quickly from a place of plenty to one of scarcity during this president's tenure. The board has instructed the president to bring it a balanced budget for the coming year and has told the president that the university will do no more borrowing.

A Successful, Proactive Approach
to Financial Pressures

Fortunately, not all institutions have been passive recipients of budget problems. Any number of institutions have budgeted conservatively, plugging into the budget projected numbers for enrollments and gifts that they are confident they will exceed, thereby maximizing the possibilities of surpluses. These institutions also have systematically created contingency funds and reserves.

Among such presidents, Pitzer College's president, Laura Skandera Trombley, has been unusually proactive. When she became president of Pitzer College in 2002, Pitzer was living in the shadow of the other Claremont Colleges, with many feeling as though the college was the poor cousin, local and regional in reach in contrast to the other institutions that were national and international. During the decade of Trombley's leadership, Pitzer has enjoyed a meteoric rise in its *U.S. News & World Report* ranking, going from 71st to 42nd. The college's selectivity in 2012–13 was 14 percent, making it among the twenty most selective higher education institutions in the United States. The college has raised more than $100 million and built eight new buildings, all LEED (Leadership in Energy and Environmental Design) certified (four Gold and four Platinum). I'll discuss how Pitzer accomplished all of this and the implications for governance in the final chapter.

What is especially pertinent here is that Trombley sought advice both on and off campus in terms of finances. Prior to 2008, she had listened carefully to a kitchen cabinet of business leaders and investors across the country who advised her that the economy was going to be in trouble. Then, in the fall of 2008, after consultation with the campus budget committee that included faculty, staff, students, and administrators, Trombley decided to cut Pitzer's operating budget by 5 percent in anticipation of that eventuality. On some level, she was taking a risk in that although by this point many people were worried about the economy, no one was clear about how serious the downturn would be. Had the downturn not been as serious as it turned out to be, Trombley would have been criticized for making unnecessary cuts. Because the recession did occur, that risk paid off. Because of this decision, Pitzer did not during the worst of the recession need to increase its draw from the endowment. Indeed, to my knowledge, it was the only college or university in the country to suspend endowment draw. It did not lay off any faculty or staff members. It did not cut financial aid and instead continued to meet the full need of its students.

Whatever their cause, financial pressures over time generally have a negative impact on the faculty, on governance, and on the quality of the academic programs. The next chapter will describe the impact of the growing reliance on contingent faculty, the trend toward online learning, including MOOCs, and the emergence of for-profit universities on the faculty, on governance, and on program quality.

3

The Impact on Governance of Contingent Faculty, Online Learning, and MOOCs

Changes in how higher education is being "delivered" have had unanticipated but significant consequences both for shared governance on college campuses and also for the quality of the academic programs. Specifically, these changes include the following:

- The growing reliance, for financial not academic reasons, at both public and private campuses, on contingent faculty—that is, faculty members who are not tenured or on tenure-track or who are graduate students—with the result that 75 percent of instructional faculty members are contingent faculty, the vast majority of whom are part-time.

- The increasing number of online courses that are taught not by regular faculty members but by those who are contracted on a course-by-course basis.

- The arrangements that some institutions (often without faculty involvement) are making with MOOCs, the massive open online courses, which sometimes also involve course-by-course teaching contracts.

- The fundamental changes that MOOCs are making to the role and nature of what it means to teach a course. For instance, the MOOCs feature a prestigious professor who provides online lectures to all the students enrolled in a course, sometimes in the tens of thousands. Student work is sometimes evaluated by people hired on a contract basis who do not have the qualifications to become faculty members. Some MOOCs don't hire people to do the grading at all, but rely on either peer grading or machine grading.

- Many online courses and MOOCs are not subject to the traditional processes for faculty review and approval of the curriculum.

Reliance on Contingent Faculty Affects Governance

Although many contingent faculty members are highly qualified with credentials equal to tenured and tenure-track faculty, they generally earn salaries that are in no way comparable to those of the tenured and tenure-track faculty, even though they often are teaching the same courses. Contingent faculty also typically receive no benefits, are often hired just before the beginning of the academic term, and usually do not have job security. They often do not have private offices, clerical support, access to technology, or even in some cases e-mail accounts. Generally, contingent faculty do not advise students and are not eligible for faculty development and travel funds.

Institutions typically do not hire or evaluate contingent faculty members in ways that are comparable to hiring and evaluation practices for tenure-track faculty. Most contingent faculty, particularly part-time adjuncts, are hired by department chairs, whereas tenure-track faculty are selected after a national search by a committee generally comprising faculty in the field who recommend the appointment to the department chair, who in turn makes a recommendation to the chief academic officer. Many contingent faculty members are not evaluated for their teaching, and in almost all cases they are not expected to do service or produce scholarship.

The growth in the percentage of contingent faculty is significant. According to the *AAUP 2011–12 Report on the Economic Status of the Profession*:

> The proportion of tenured and tenure-track faculty members shrank dramatically between 1975 and 2009, from more than 45 percent to less than 25 percent. In all, graduate student employees and faculty members serving in contingent appointments now make up more than 75 percent of the total instructional staff. The most rapid growth has been among part-time faculty members, whose numbers swelled by more than 280 percent between 1975 and 2009 (pp. 10–11).

In real terms, this means that more than 1 million out of approximately 1.5 million faculty members in the United States are now contingent faculty.

The growing reliance on contingent faculty, while financially advantageous to hiring institutions, has undermined and will increasingly undermine the practice of shared governance. Specifically, because contingent faculty generally do not serve on departmental or institutional committees, do not have a role in the hiring process, do not participate in the performance reviews of their colleagues, and do not have a vote on such matters as the curriculum and academic standards, most college and university faculty today do not participate in governance in any meaningful way if at all.

The implications of the exclusion of the majority of the teaching faculty from shared governance are several. The institutions that hire them, their students, and their colleagues are deprived of these faculty members' perspective and contributions, despite the fact that they may be teaching a preponderance of students on that campus. Contingent faculty members are also apt to feel alienated from and even exploited by the institutions that hire them, something that is not good for the contingent faculty members, their students, or their institutions. Most of all, this practice diminishes the quality of the educational experience that colleges and universities are providing students—through, I hasten to emphasize, no fault of most of the contingent faculty.

Reliance on Contingent Faculty Can Compromise Educational Quality

Because many contingent faculty members are hired at the last moment, they do not have adequate time to prepare their classes. They certainly do not have the luxury that tenured and tenure-track faculty members have of the summer months to prepare new courses. They also are often not available to their students other than before and after class and during office hours. Because many contingent faculty members, particularly the majority who are part-time, do not get to know their full-time colleagues, they are typically not part of the dialogue about teaching and learning, about the curriculum, and about advances in their discipline that tends to be part of the life of full-time faculty.

The institutions and their students suffer because many very capable and committed people, by virtue of the way their positions are structured, do not become part of the life of the campus and do not develop the one-on-one relationships with their students that so many colleges celebrate. Moreover, because contingent faculty members typically receive much lower pay than tenure and tenure-track faculty, in order to earn a living wage, they often cobble together a slate of courses at several institutions. Contingent faculty who live in major urban areas joke that their only office is their car.

This arrangement is not limited to larger or public institutions. For example, a well-regarded liberal arts college whose tuition, room, and board are well above $50,000 a year posts on its website that more than half of its several hundred faculty members are part-time adjuncts. Nearly 45 percent of all courses on this campus are taught by adjuncts. Although students at this college praise some of the adjuncts, others complain that these professors are seldom available other than before and after class and during their few office hours every week. Some students reportedly have transferred, questioning why they should pay such a high tuition when they could take classes from the same faculty members at the neighboring community college at a fraction of the cost.

In their August 2012 Center for the Future of Higher Education study of 500 contingent faculty members, *Who Is Professor "Staff"—and How Can This Person Teach So Many Classes?*, Steve Street, Maria Maisto, Esther Merves, and Gary Rhoades reported the following statistics:

- 77 percent of respondents teach in part-time, contingent positions

- 54 percent teach in more than one institution

- 29 percent teach in two institutions

- 11 percent teach in three institutions

- 6 percent teach in four institutions

Fourteen percent also teach in both two- and four-year institutions, which may have a different mix of students and different expectations for their courses.

In short, contingent faculty who are paid only to teach their classes and hold office hours in a very real sense become pieceworkers.

There are some important exceptions to what I've just written about contingent faculty. In some disciplines, hiring practitioners as adjuncts serves students especially well and gives practitioners interested in teaching an opportunity to do so. For example, at the University of Puget Sound, we were very fortunate to be able to hire extremely talented musicians from the Seattle and Tacoma symphonies to give lessons to our students. The same is true, for example, for the other arts, for business, for law, and for health sciences.

It is also the case that many practitioners teach as an add-on to their normal professional life, where they are apt to have the benefits of colleagueship and of a full-time salary. Their circumstances are very different from those faculty whose only livelihood is teaching and who are hired at reduced compensation, often at the last minute, to teach classes.

Adjuncts Receive Significantly Lower Compensation

The Adjunct Project, an online effort that involves crowdsourcing and with which the *Chronicle of Higher Education* is collaborating, has studied the disparity of adjunct pay among institutions. Audrey Williams June and Jonah Newman, in their January 4, 2013 *Chronicle of Higher Education* piece, "Adjunct Project Reveals Wide Range in Pay," provide the following data:

> The overall average pay reported by adjuncts is $2,987 per three-credit course. Adjuncts at 16 colleges reported earning less than $1,000. The highest pay reported is $12,575, in the anthropology department at Harvard University.
>
> The data document how it pays, literally, for adjuncts to teach at top research universities, where they report receiving an average of $4,750 per three-credit course. Yet even within that category, pay differs widely. The average per-course pay reported for adjuncts at Ohio State University is $4,853, compared with an average of $6,500 reported at the University of Michigan at Ann Arbor. Harvard pays adjuncts $11,037, on average, according to the data that adjuncts have submitted so far.
>
> Meanwhile, adjuncts at rural, medium-sized, two-year institutions—where pay is the lowest, according to the data submitted so far—average $1,808 per three-credit course.

Some institutions are now limiting the number of hours adjuncts teach in order to avoid having to provide them with health benefits, as the Affordable Health Care Act will mandate in 2014. For example, the May 26, 2013 *Plain Dealer* (Cleveland, Ohio) reported that beginning in the fall of 2013, the University of Akron would limit part-time instructors to eight credit hours per semester. Faced with a $26.7 million deficit, Akron's provost, Mike Sherman, says the university simply cannot afford the more than $4 million that providing their roughly one thousand adjuncts with health care would cost. Instead, the Akron plans to hire two hundred additional adjuncts, limiting them to eight credit hours.

Contingent Faculty Are Often Considered Second Class

At many institutions, contingent faculty are considered second class by the administration and sometimes by tenured and tenure-track faculty, again through no circumstance of the contingent faculty's own making.

Morehouse University, for example, created a public relations problem for itself when it ruled that adjunct faculty would not be given tickets for the June 2013 commencement ceremony at which President Obama was speaking. After a public outcry, the university agreed to give each adjunct one ticket but did not allow them to sit with the tenured and tenure-track faculty.

Sociology professor Ivan Evans at the University of California-San Diego goes so far as to berate his tenured and tenure-track colleagues as being like Brahmins ignoring the plight of the untouchables. In his essay, "When Adjunct Faculty Are the Tenure-Track's Untouchables," quoted in Christopher Newfield's May 19, 2013 entry on the blog *Remaking the University*, Professor Evans argues:

It is the norm for adjuncts to be excluded from faculty meetings and to be deprived of any say in the management of departments. Instead of resisting the "adjunctification" of the professoriate by incorporating these colleagues—because they are colleagues—into the university and our respective departments, we tolerate them as useful proof of our Brahmin status. They are our untouchables.

Faculty Tensions About the Role of Contingent Faculty

The decisions about salary, benefits, and offices for contingent faculty generally are administrative decisions. The tenure-track and tenured faculty are, for their part, apt to deplore the fact that their compensation is significantly more than their adjunct counterparts, again often for teaching the same courses. In addition, most faculty members that I know would welcome additional tenure-track faculty to their department or program. Nevertheless, on many campuses it is the tenured and tenure-track faculty, not the administration, who prohibit the participation of contingent faculty in matters of governance, for reasons I will discuss later. As a result, the question of the role of contingent faculty in governance has created tensions within the faculty at some institutions.

For example, in March 2013 the faculty of the College of Arts and Sciences at New York University voted to deny voting privileges in faculty meetings to full-time non-tenure-line faculty, something they had always previously approved. A month later, the Professional Staff Congress at the City University of New York, the union representing more than 25,000 faculty members, ruled that only full-time faculty members (mainly tenure and tenure-track) would be allowed to participate in a planned vote of no confidence in a program that centered around transferring students from community colleges to four-year colleges. Scott Jaschik, in an April 29, 2013 *Inside Higher Ed* article, "Union Democracy for Some?," reports that the part-time faculty members, who teach many of the community colleges' courses, were "furious."

Complexities Associated with the Role of Contingent Faculty in Governance

Even though I join those who deplore the way that contingent faculty are compensated and treated, the question of the role of their involvement in governance is complicated. On the one hand, the AAUP argues that every member of the teaching faculty, including contingent faculty, should have full voting rights. On the other hand, some tenured and tenure-track faculty oppose this notion of "one person, one vote," arguing that because the roles and responsibilities of contingent faculty are different, they should not be given full voting rights.

AAUP Recommendations for Contingent Faculty

The AAUP directly addressed the role of contingent faculty in terms of governance in a January 2013 report, *The Inclusion in Governance of Faculty Members Holding Contingent Appointments*.

The AAUP recommended that faculty be included in "governance bodies at all levels," including

> individuals whose appointments consist primarily of teaching or research activities conducted at a professional level. These include (1) tenured faculty, (2) tenure-track faculty, (3) full- and part-time non-tenure-track teachers, (4) graduate-student employees and postdoctoral fellows who are primarily teachers or researchers, and (5) librarians who participate substantially in the process of teaching or research. Those individuals whose primary duties are administrative should not be defined as faculty.

The AAUP further called for contingent faculty to be given the opportunity to review other contingent faculty members and to "be eligible to vote in all elections for institutional governance bodies on the basis of one person, one vote." The AAUP recommended that contingent faculty should also be protected from retaliation and should be compensated in a way that takes into consideration the full range of their appointment responsibilities, which should include service.

Arguments Against Voting Rights for Contingent Faculty

Many faculty members and administrators oppose the AAUP recommendations about voting rights for contingent faculty, arguing that the roles and responsibilities of tenured and tenure-track faculty are very different from those of contingent faculty. For example, in addition to teaching, the formal responsibilities of the tenured and tenure-track faculty include scholarship and service. In contrast, as noted earlier, contingent faculty members are not expected to produce scholarship (or rewarded if they do so), nor are they expected or often allowed to provide service. It is also the case that tenured and tenure-track faculty undergo a more rigorous, comprehensive, and regular review process and are likely, simply because of the way their responsibilities are defined, to have a greater in-depth knowledge of the institution.

Some tenured and tenure-track faculty also resist giving voting rights to contingent faculty on the ground that because contingent faculty do not have job security, they might be more prone to pressure from both the administration and also tenured faculty members to vote in certain ways than faculty with job security would be. The same argument is often made in terms of whether tenure-track faculty should participate fully in governance matters prior to earning tenure.

Contingent Faculty Organize

In recent years, contingent faculty have begun to organize, forming groups like the New Faculty Majority, which estimates that adjuncts now number a million or more people. Increasing numbers are also unionizing. For example, 72 percent of the approximately

200 adjuncts at Georgetown University voted to unionize in May 2013. They joined the majority of the 2,400 adjuncts at other D.C. institutions, including George Washington University, American University, and Montgomery College, who had previously become members of the Service Employees International Union (SEIU) Local 500. Fourteen months later, SEIU began an effort to organize contingent faculty colleges in Boston. The United Steelworkers did the same in Pittsburgh.

This movement almost certainly will affect how governance is practiced on some campuses. For example, although different groups of adjunct faculty have different priorities, their common goals generally include better compensation and more job security. SEIU, for example, is pushing for benefits and pay packages comparable to those of tenured and tenure-track faculty. Achieving this would in turn have an impact on how resources are allocated and how non-tenure-track faculty positions will be defined and filled.

Some contingent faculty members are also advocating a citywide approach for hiring. For example, Annie McLeer, who directs the SEIU's campaign to organize adjuncts on 500 campuses, has advocated creating citywide bargaining units and collaboration among the colleges and universities in terms of hiring that might include centralized job posting or even replicate something like a union hiring hall. If several colleges and universities within the same city adopted this approach, it too would inevitably have an impact on governance with participating institutions almost certainly needing to create new policies and practices in terms of hiring, course scheduling, evaluation, and compensation.

Joe Berry, author of the 2005 Monthly Review Press book *Reclaiming the Ivory Tower: Organizing Adjuncts to Change Higher Education*, believes that citywide bargaining would give adjuncts significant power: "They could shut down the universities with a credible strike threat, because they teach most of the classes."

The Modern Language Association Recommendations for Contingent Faculty

The Modern Language Association (MLA), the professional organization for faculty in English and foreign languages, has recommended an approach to compensation to its member institutions: "minimum compensation for 2011–12 of $6,800 for a standard 3-credit-hour semester course or $4,530 for a standard 3-credit-hour quarter or trimester course . . . based on a full-time load of 3 courses per semester (6 per year) or 3 courses per quarter or trimester (9 per year)." What this would mean is that full-time contingent faculty would receive a salary of just shy of $41,000. Yet, according to data that past MLA president Michael Bérubé reported in the Modern Language Association president's blog entry of March 30, 2011, "From the President: Among the Majority," only 7 percent of member institutions were meeting or exceeding those recommendations.

Institutional Responses to Contingent Faculty Unions

Some institutions, like Georgetown and American University, have not challenged the efforts of their contingent faculty to unionize. Others have done so.

For example, Duquesne University and Pacific Lutheran University (PLU) each argued that because they were religious institutions (Roman Catholic and Lutheran respectively), they did not fall under the jurisdiction of the National Labor Relations Board. In June 2012, the NLRB ruled in favor of Duquesne's 130 adjuncts, who comprise half the teaching faculty. A year later, the NLRB ruled in favor of the contingent faculty at PLU, where one-third of all credit hours are taught by 39 full-time and 137 part-time contingent faculty, enabling them to vote on unionizing.

Recommendation: Move Contingent Faculty to Ongoing, Full-Time Positions

Although I understand the financial pressures that lead colleges and universities to hire adjuncts and other contingent faculty,

I believe strongly that colleges and universities as much as is possible should seek to reverse the trend toward contingent rather than full-time ongoing faculty and should compensate those who are contract employees in ways that are not exploitive. Doing so will, I believe, serve both students and contingent faculty. Doing so will also be true to the values that so many colleges and universities today embrace as they commit to notions of fairness and social justice. I also believe that doing so might prove to be cost-neutral or even cost-effective.

My logic is this:

Most colleges and universities today understand the benefits to the institution of improved retention in terms of both additional enrollment, which provides increased tuition, and often also increased revenues for room and board. Retaining a current student also is far less expensive than recruiting a new student.

I expect that having more full-time ongoing faculty who are available to their students beyond classroom time and office hours and who have become part of the life of the campus will improve retention. In fact, a recent study confirms the importance of every individual professor on student choices. In this case, Daniel F. Chambliss and Christopher G. Takacs, in a chapter from their forthcoming Harvard University Press book, *How College Works*, report that individual professors in the first courses students take determine whether students are interested in majoring in that particular field or become altogether alienated from it. It is not much of a leap to conclude that the same phenomenon has an impact on whether a student decides to remain at or transfer from the institution.

Depending on the level of tuition, retaining even a few students would cover the additional salary to make one adjunct faculty member a full-time one.

Even if these new positions were not tenure-track positions but contract positions of several years' duration, I would encourage involving those holding these positions in both governance and service, thereby bringing their important perspectives and experiences to bear on matters of institutional importance and also lessening the service expectations for tenured and tenure-track faculty, freeing them to devote more of their time to teaching, advising students, and scholarship.

Online Courses and MOOCs

Over the past several years, some new approaches to online learning, including MOOCs, have attracted significant investors and substantial public attention with the promise that they would provide a cost-effective approach to education. The MOOCs in particular claimed the ability to reach students around the world who would not otherwise have access to the quality of education that the MOOCs presumed to offer. Tamar Levin, in the July 17, 2012 *New York Times* article, "Universities Reshaping Education on the Web," referred to MOOCs as part of "a seismic shift in online learning that is reshaping higher education."

MOOCs began to attract international attention in 2011 when Stanford professors Sebastian Thrun and Peter Norvig offered one of the first MOOCs, a free course on artificial intelligence online. After fifty-eight thousand people signed up for this course, Thrun formed his own company, Udacity. That same year, two other Stanford professors, Daphne Koller and Andrew Ng, founded Coursera, enrolling hundreds of thousands of students across the globe in courses developed in partnership with faculty from some of the country's major research universities.

Inspired by writers like Christensen and Eyring, even though no one had yet actually implemented a financially successful business model for MOOCs, investors put up tens of millions of dollars for these and other new companies. Many of the nation's most prestigious institutions entered into partnerships with these new companies. In addition, a great many institutions are now themselves seriously exploring ways to use online learning with the goal of reducing costs, creating new revenue streams, or increasing access to the education that they offer.

Although liberal arts faculty have historically been particularly skeptical about this approach to education, institutions as prestigious as Wellesley and Wesleyan have now entered into agreements with edX and Coursera. In contrast, as I will discuss later, the faculty at equally prestigious institutions like Amherst and Duke have prevented their institutions from partnering with some of these new firms.

Many boards of trustees, like the board at Virginia, have encouraged their presidents actively to embrace MOOCs and other forms of online learning. I think it fair to say that this phenomenon of free online learning is preoccupying many institutions, large and small, public and private, as they try to determine how to incorporate online learning into conventional classes. This question is particularly challenging for those small private colleges and honors programs in flagship universities that have prided themselves on providing their students with individual attention. These colleges struggle with the question of whether and if so how they can become both "high-tech" by, for example, developing hybrid courses, and remain "high-touch" by continuing to emphasize personalized student-faculty interactions.

The American Council on Education has taken a particularly proactive role among higher education associations, working with firms like Coursera, Udacity, edX, and others, as ACE announces on its website, "to identify and answer questions about the disruptive potential of this new and innovative approach to higher education." For example, ACE has created what it calls the "Presidential Innovation Lab," a think tank of fourteen college presidents, funded by the Bill and Melinda Gates Foundation, to "consider questions such as how newer educational innovations could be used by students toward degree completion and the potential impact of such innovations on the fundamental design and delivery of instruction, institutions' recognition of learning, and the underlying financing models for all of higher education." ACE has recommended that colleges give credit to some MOOCs offered by these companies.

The Impact of MOOCs on Governance

The impact of MOOCs on governance has already occurred. On some campuses, the administration has signed contracts with companies for courses without involving the faculty in the decision-making process, thereby no longer giving primary responsibility for the curriculum to the faculty of each of these institutions. Ry Rivard, in a July 17, 2013 *Inside Higher Ed* piece, "No-Bid MOOCs," reports that "at least 21 universities and higher education systems in 16 states have signed agreements with Coursera, Udacity or edX without going through a competitive bidding process," thereby potentially diverting "untold amounts of taxpayer or student tuition money to outside vendors."

In addition, faculty members teaching online courses to thousands or even hundreds of thousands of students rather than just those in their real-time, real-place classroom are now entering into new sorts of contractual relationships with their home institution and increasingly with other institutions. Going forward, some faculty members will rely on (or be required to rely on) online course modules developed by others, and some will move to the role of leading discussions among their students about these modules rather than being the primary or only instructor. Such changes in faculty responsibilities are likely in turn to lead to redefinitions of faculty workload, faculty compensation, and perhaps the contractual relationship of faculty members with the institution for which they work. MOOCs and other online courses therefore raise fundamental questions about what historically has been the role of faculty members.

Stephen P. Balfour, in an undated piece on the Research and Practice in Assessment (RPA) website, "Assessing Writing in MOOCs: Automated Essay Scoring and Calibrated Peer Review™," reported that grading, for example, for edX, MIT and Harvard's nonprofit MOOC federation, is done by a "machine-based Automated Essay Scoring (AES) application." Coursera for its part prefers to use peer grading rather than hiring real faculty to assess student writing. In addition to questions about the reliability of machine and peer grading, there also is the reality that grading—historically a critical faculty responsibility—no longer resides with the faculty but either with a machine or with the students themselves.

Other faculty members, like those at Amherst, question the impact on the quality of student-faculty interaction of incorporating online learning into conventional classes.

Faculty Concerns About MOOCS

Duke University

Duke University drew headlines in April 2013 when its Arts and Sciences Council voted against the university's arrangement with 2U, thereby effectively ending the relationship. (Duke, however, does continue to work with Coursera.) Under the agreement with 2U, Duke and nine other prominent universities would have created a "pool of for-credit online classes for undergraduates" for the program known as Semester Online. Students would receive credit for these courses, which would include blended learning—that is, both online learning featuring recorded lectures and also in-person discussions led by a real person, often a graduate student.

The Duke faculty reportedly was concerned about 2U on several levels. They opposed the notion that students who had not been accepted as regular Duke students nevertheless would receive Duke credit for these courses. Some also opposed the fact that Duke students would receive credit for courses offered by institutions that these faculty members did not see as being of Duke's caliber.

Amherst

Amherst president Carolyn (Biddy) Martin left to the faculty the decision whether Amherst should join edX, a nonprofit consortium of roughly a dozen prestigious institutions founded by Harvard and the Massachusetts Institute of Technology (MIT) to create MOOCs.

The Amherst faculty then voted down an offer from edX, arguing that MOOCs ran counter to the college's commitment to "learning through close colloquy" and instead might "perpetuate the 'information dispensing' model of teaching" and also potentially "create the conditions for the obsolescence of the B.A. degree." Some Amherst faculty members also worried that edX would offer certificates of completion bearing Amherst's name and that student work would be graded by machines and include multiple choice exams, which are anathema to Amherst faculty. Some additionally worried that the need to be profitable might lead edX and the consortium to make decisions that ran counter to the values of the academy.

San Jose State

Members of the philosophy department at San Jose State refused to teach an edX course on social justice because, as they wrote to the course's creator, Harvard's Michael Sandel, in an open letter, they feared that doing so would encourage a movement to "replace professors, dismantle departments, and provide a diminished education for students in public universities." In an eloquent statement, these faculty members make the case for the value of classes taught by faculty who have themselves done research in the topic, who have done scholarship in the area they are teaching, and who engage the topic with their students passionately and "deeply, thoroughly and analytically in a dynamic and up-to-date fashion."

The San Jose philosophy professors also feared "that two classes of universities will be created: one, well-funded colleges and universities in which privileged students get their own real professor; the other, financially stressed private and public universities in which students watch a bunch of videotaped lectures and interact, if indeed any interaction is available on their home campuses, with a professor that this model of education has turned into a glorified teaching assistant."

In short, in addition to their concerns about the quality of instruction via MOOCs, the San Jose professors saw MOOCs as undermining shared governance and the way that many colleges and universities have organized themselves around the disciplines in which the faculty have been educated, have teaching experience, and conduct scholarship.

Harvard Faculty of Arts and Sciences

Fifty-eight members of Harvard University's Faculty of Arts and Sciences (FAS), soon after the statement from the San Jose philosophers, similarly expressed their concerns in an open letter to their dean about "the costs and consequences" of edX and Harvard X and also about the "impact on line courses will have on higher education as a whole." Like the faculty at Duke, the Harvard arts and science faculty members were concerned that they had not been sufficiently involved in the conversations about the proposed online programs. The dean denied their request to have a new committee of FAS "ladder" faculty develop a set of ethical and educational principles that would govern Harvard X, saying that he intended instead to work with the committees that were already in operation and that had FAS representation but also included faculty from across the university.

The Provosts at the University of Chicago and Big Ten Universities

This group of provosts from the Committee on Institutional Cooperation, whose member institutions provide roughly one-sixth of Coursera's courses, released a position paper in June 2013 also challenging the hype about MOOCs and expressing the worry that MOOCs might lead corporations rather than universities to determine the future of higher education.

Concerns About MOOCs Beyond the Academy

It is not only faculty who have raised a number of questions about the efficacy of MOOCs and who have argued that MOOCs may diluting the quality of education. For example, Jason Boyers, in a July 4, 2013 Huffington Post piece, "Why MOOCs Miss the Point with Online Learning," said that students enrolling in MOOCs have been completing the courses at very low rates. For example, only 7 percent of those enrolling in Thrun and Norvig's artificial intelligence course completed it, compared to the 80–90 percent of students who complete an online course in which they work closely with a professor. What makes this number even more stunning is, as Robinson Meyer reports in his July 18, 2012 *Atlantic* essay, "What It's Like to Teach a MOOC (and What the Heck's a MOOC)," that most of those who signed up for the class were already highly educated, with reportedly 60 percent of them employed in the information technology industry.

MOOCs have also not yet lived up to their promise of being an attractive low-cost option for students to earn college credit. For example, by the summer of 2013, not one student had signed on to the offer from Colorado State University-Global Campus for credit to students who completed a Udacity MOOC in computer science and then passed a proctored exam, which would cost $89 even though the university charged $1,050 for the comparable traditional course. Similarly, no student has turned to the Learning-Counts Program at the Council of Adult and Experiential Learning for help in creating portfolios of online learning in order to be awarded course credit.

MOOCs have also turned out to be costly rather than inexpensive. edX, for instance, will help institutions develop courses for $250,000 per course and charges an additional $50,000 each time the course is offered.

Some faculty are also concerned about the impact of MOOCs on faculty time. In this regard, Steven Kolowich reports in an April 29, 2017 *Chronicle of Higher Ed* piece that a recent survey revealed "that professors typically spent 100 hours, sometimes much more, to develop their massive online courses, and then eight to 10 hours each week while the courses were in session. This commitment amounted to a major drain on their normal campus responsibilities."

In the summer of 2013, a number of organizations and individuals that had been wholeheartedly supporting MOOCs began to raise concerns of their own. For instance, Ry Rivard in a July 9, 2013 *Inside Higher Ed* piece, "Beyond MOOC Hype," reports that "Dan Greenstein, the head of postsecondary success at the Bill & Melinda Gates Foundation, now wonders aloud if MOOCs are a 'viable thing or are just a passing fad.'" Despite the fact that the Gates Foundation has committed $3 million for grants related to MOOCS, Greenstein remarked, "higher ed is suffering from 'innovation exhaustion,' and MOOCs are part of the problem."

Rivard further reports that "ACE President Molly Corbett Broad said the free online classes have perhaps been greeted with more hype than is appropriate" and that "now is the time for us to step back and do what all of us at universities are the best at doing: criticizing or evaluating or recommending changes or improvements—or some will choose to walk away from this strategy altogether."

Recommendation: Institutions Should Be Clear About Processes for MOOCs and Other Online Courses

I am not here recommending a specific process for each and every campus, because circumstances are different at different institutions. What I do recommend, however, is that there be absolute clarity about who has the responsibility and authority for hiring and evaluating those who teach these courses and for approving the courses themselves.

One model that I have seen work would be akin to the model that many colleges and universities already use when they offer graduate programs—that is, certain faculty are designated graduate faculty and provide the oversight role for the graduate programs. Those who teach only undergraduate courses are not involved in these processes. Other institutions have created separate structures for professional programs, whether they are undergraduate, graduate level, or both. Institutions might also create an organizational entity responsible for online programs, separate from conventional classes. However, I would argue that blended classes, which combine the conventional classroom experience with some online components, would need to be reviewed and approved by the peers of the faculty teaching those courses.

But whatever the process, I think there needs to be a logic to it. It needs to be consistent with the institution's governing documents. And ultimately, there needs to be great clarity about who is responsible for and has authority for what.

For-Profit Universities

For-profit institutions, which often rely on online courses, have in the past decades attracted their share of students, some of whom might not have previously attended college, but many others who would have in an earlier era chosen brick-and-mortar campuses. The latter case has been particularly characteristic of those seeking degrees in education at the undergraduate and graduate levels. For example, an August 7, 2012 USA Today piece, "Online Education Degrees Skyrocket," reported that in 2011 the University of Phoenix Online gave out 5,975 degrees in education, compared to the 72 degrees they awarded a decade ago. In that same year, Walden gave education degrees to 4,878 students, Grand Canyon University awarded 4,822 such degrees, and National University gave out 4,669 education degrees.

For-profit institutions, like MOOCs, initially attracted a good deal of attention. Almost none of these institutions grant tenure to faculty and instead hire most of their teachers on a course-by-course contract basis without benefits. For-profit institutions don't pretend to involve faculty in governance but rather are run as corporations that hire contract employees as needed. In fact, the Integrated Postsecondary Education Data System (IPEDS) reported that in 2011 only 18 percent of the employees at these institutions were categorized as faculty. For these reasons, some early investors believed that for-profit online education would be the panacea for rising costs. That has not proven to be the case.

Instead, many online and for-profit institutions today are under attack because of their high loan default rate, high levels of attrition, and misleading recruiting practices. For example, Mary Nguyen, in the *Degreeless in Debt: What Happens to Borrowers Who Drop Out* (Education Sector 2012) reported the following concerning trends:

> Student borrowing has increased to the point that a majority of freshmen at all institutions now borrow to pay for their education. Borrowing has grown the most at for-profit institutions. This is especially significant because for-profit institutions enroll just 9 percent of all college students.

> While borrowing is on the rise, dropout rates are also increasing. For-profit, four-year institutions have the highest dropout rate. In 2009, 54 percent of students in these institutions dropped out, an increase of 20 percentage points from 2001, when the rate was 34 percent.

These factors, along with the often high tuition that for-profit institutions charge, have led the industry leader, the University of Phoenix, among others, to encounter enrollment and financial problems. In early 2013, according to the Associated Press, the Apollo Group announced that in the last quarter of fiscal year 2012, it saw a 60 percent decline in net income. As a consequence, Phoenix announced that it would close 115 of its smaller locations, which would affect 13,000 students. Phoenix also announced that it would reduce expenses by $300 million, or 9 percent, and eliminate 800 nonfaculty positions.

As with the MOOCs and other online programs, at least to date, for-profit institutions have also not lived up to the hype that these alternatives to more traditional colleges and universities would achieve efficiencies, in great part because their faculties tended to comprise contract employees who were not involved in governance and whose compensation was less.

The next chapter will first describe the growing questions on the part of families, the general public, and elected officials about whether a college education offers enough value to warrant its high cost and then explore the ways that these questions have altered how governance is practiced on many campuses.

4

The Impact on Governance of Questions About Higher Education's Value and Cost

In recent years, a series of writers, a great many elected officials, the American Council of Trustees and Alumni (ACTA), and others have attacked higher education in several significant ways. The arguments include the following:

- The benefits of a college education do not justify its costs.

- A liberal arts curriculum no longer serves the needs of the larger society; public colleges and universities in particular should emphasize areas of study that will lead to immediate jobs.

- Remedial education is not effective, and therefore the states should not fund it at public institutions.

- Graduation rates at many institutions, particularly those in the public sector, are so low that funding these institutions makes no sense.

- Students are not really learning very much.

- A college education is not necessary for success. Among those making this argument, it has become a cliché that the achievements of Steve Jobs, Bill Gates, and Mark Zuckerberg, the first of whom dropped out of Reed and the other two out of Harvard, demonstrate that a college education is not necessary even though most college dropouts do not typically enjoy the success of college graduates, both economic and personal.

As I will discuss later in this chapter, such attacks have led both elected officials and trustees to seek to influence both the curriculum and also how education is being "delivered" to students in unprecedented ways and often without any deference at all being given to faculty perspectives. There is a great deal of evidence that a college education benefits graduates both economically and personally, something that frequently gets ignored in the often hyperbolic rhetoric.

Higher Education Is Vulnerable to Criticism

To be sure, there is much to criticize about higher education. In addition to rising costs, the public is right to be concerned about low graduation rates at some institutions, the growing amount of debt students and their families are incurring, and the lowering of standards and expectations for students across the sector.

Graduation Rates

The standard calculation for graduate rates, based on data from the Integrated Postsecondary Education Data System (IPEDS), provides only limited information. As Bryan Cook and Terry Hartle point out on the ACE spring/summer 2010 website, "IPEDS counts only those students who enroll in an institution as full-time degree-seekers and finish a degree at the same institution within a prescribed period of time." In other words, the "IPEDS calculation excludes students who begin college part time, who enroll mid-year, and who transfer from one institution to another." Valencia College president Stanford Shugart, in a speech that he gave to the Southern Association of Colleges and Schools' Commission on Colleges, provided evidence that the difference in how graduation rates are calculated can have an enormous effect on the outcome. Specifically, he reported that the published graduation rate at Austin Community College was

3.9 percent. When, however, the completion rate includes either graduation or transferring to another institution, the percentage jumped to 43 percent. Nevertheless, the IPEDS calculation is the one used by U.S. News & World Report in its college rankings, by most colleges in their publicity, and by state legislatures in making funding decisions.

Despite these limitations, the IPEDS data reveal how widely graduation rates vary across institutions, regions, and sectors. For example, at some of the country's most prestigious institutions, most of the students who enroll as freshmen do in fact graduate in six years. (Although most traditional colleges offer four-year programs, because many students take longer than that to graduate, a six-year graduation rate is usually the standard for comparison.) For example, the six-year graduation rate at Harvard and Yale is 98 percent and at Princeton 97 percent. The top liberal arts colleges too have impressive six-year graduation rates: Williams at 96 percent, Pomona at 95 percent, and Amherst and Bowdoin at 94 percent.

The picture is not as promising at many other schools. The National Center of Education Statistics reported that only "approximately 58 percent of first-time, full-time students who began seeking a bachelor's degree at a 4-year institution in fall 2004 completed a bachelor's degree at that institution within 6 years." The rates were highest for private nonprofits (65 percent) compared with public institutions (56 percent) and private for-profits (28 percent).

Graduation rates for some individual institutions, as calculated by IPEDS, are shockingly low. For example, in 2011, only 4 percent of entering full-time students at Southern University at New Orleans graduated in six years, and only 7.7 percent at the University of the District of Columbia did. Some branch campuses of some larger public universities also have dismal graduation rates. At Kent State at East Liverpool, only 8.9 percent of full-time freshmen graduated in six years. At Ohio University's Southern campus in Ironton, the number is 13.7 percent, and at Purdue's North Central campus, 14 percent. Indeed, concerns about the graduation rates at North Central and its neighboring Purdue Calumet (34 miles

away), compared to the 70 percent graduation rate at the main
Purdue campus, led Indiana governor Mitch Daniels, shortly after
he was named the next president of Purdue, to comment publicly,
"Some kids run up some bills and don't even get through."

State Legislatures Base Funding on IPEDS-Based Graduation Rates

Despite the fact that graduation rates, or as they now are often
called "completion" rates, calculated with IPEDS data do not take
into account the growing numbers of students who enroll part-time
or who transfer to and graduate from another institution, state legislatures across the country are basing funding on these rates.

The organization Complete College America, for example,
has received funding from such foundations as Gates, Lumina,
Carnegie Corporation, Ford, and Kellogg, as well as the federal
government, to encourage state legislatures to institute policies
designed to increase graduation rates. By February 2013, twelve
states (Illinois, Indiana, Louisiana, Michigan, Minnesota, New
Mexico, Ohio, Oklahoma, Pennsylvania, South Dakota, Tennessee,
and Washington) had, according to the National Conference of
State Legislatures (NCSL), based funding on such criteria as
the number of degrees awarded generally, the number of degrees
awarded to low-income and minority students, course completion,
transfer rates, and time to degree. NCSL is particularly focused on
finding ways to enable students to avoid remedial courses and to
encourage colleges and universities to come up with innovative
approaches to remediation.

This emphasis on completion has caused a fair amount of con-
sternation among faculty members in these states, who worry that
this approach to funding will lead to diminishing requirements or
will encourage faculty members to give passing grades to more students in order to secure funding. Such diminishing of academic
standards and of academic quality of course defeats the very purpose

of the "completion agenda," which is to bring more well educated Americans into the workforce.

There is also the irony that many of the same state legislatures that are basing funding on graduation rates include those that have reduced funding for the public institutions. These reductions in funds have inevitably required students to work greater numbers of hours outside of class. Not unexpectedly, there is a correlation between hours worked and academic performance. For example, the 2012 National Study on Student Engagement (NSSE) research showed that slightly more than a third of students employed between 6 and 20 hours per week and 60 percent of students employed more than 20 hours per week believed that their employment had a negative impact on their academic performance.

In other words, state legislatures have now interjected themselves into the academic arena, substituting their judgment for that of the faculty and administrators at the public institutions in their states.

Student Debt

Both those students who graduate from college and those who drop out often incur huge debt. Nguyen, in *Degreeless in Debt*, reported that debt hits hardest the 30 percent of students who take out loans and then drop out of school. Understandably, those who do not graduate are four times more likely to default on their college loans than are graduates.

According to the June 2013 Urban Institute report, "Forever in Your Debt: Who Has Student Loan Debt, and Who's Worried?," thirty-eight million students in the summer of 2013 owed more than a trillion dollars for student loans, a number four times what it was a decade ago. Not surprisingly, the majority (57 percent) worries about their ability to repay their loans. This question of student debt has entered the political arena, and only after much contentiousness in August 2013 did Congress pass and President

Obama sign a bill that would tie interest rates for student loans to the financial markets.

Diminished Academic Standards

Colleges and universities are also suffering from grade inflation that begins at the high school level. The UCLA Higher Education Research Institute's annual study of first-year students released in 2011 revealed that 47.5 percent of college freshmen reported that they had A averages in high school. Only 4.2 percent had C averages and the rest were in the B range. Interestingly, 71 percent of first-year students considered themselves to be either in the top 10 percent or at least above average when it came to academic ability.

It is not that these students are studying harder or learning more than in the past. Rather, the survey shows that high school students are today studying far fewer hours than was the case several decades ago. For example, 60 percent of college freshmen reported studying five or fewer hours per week when they were in high school. The trend continues at least through the first year of college. The 2012 NSSE survey reported that the average first-year student studies fifteen hours per week (which is several hours fewer than faculty believe they are studying).

Retired Duke professor Stuart Rojstaczer and Furman professor Christopher Healy, in their piece in *Teacher's College Record*, "Where A Is Ordinary: The Evolution of American College and University Grading, 1940–2009," report that grade inflation is increasingly rampant at the college level:

> On average across a wide range of schools, A's represent 43% of all letter grades, an increase of 28 percentage points since 1960 and 12 percentage points since 1988. D's and F's total typically less than 10% of all letter grades. . . . At schools with modest selectivity, grading is as generous as it was in the mid-1980s at highly

selective schools. These prestigious schools have, in turn, continued to ramp up their grades. It is likely that at many selective and highly selective schools, undergraduate GPAs are now so saturated at the high end that they have little use as a motivator of students and as an evaluation tool for graduate and professional schools and employers.

Claims That Colleges Are Failing to Educate Students

Skepticism about the value of higher education has been the sub-ject of several recent books, which argue that a college education as it is currently configured is not worth the cost and that both academic standards and expectations are being diminished. These works often attack the curriculum, argue that higher education does need to be disrupted and changed, and advocate the use of technol-ogy as a means to cutting costs.

Like *The Innovative University*, these books have received a good deal of attention from both elected officials and trustees, who often cite them as they attempt to influence how colleges and universities function, again often in areas that previously had been the province of the faculty.

Academically Adrift

Richard Arum and Josipa Roksa argue in *Academically Adrift: Lim-ited Learning on College Campuses* that college students don't gain important analytical skills or learn much. The authors summarized their views in a May 14, 2011 *New York Times* op-ed piece, "Your So-Called Education," this way:

> In a typical semester, for instance, 32 percent of the students did not take a single course with more than 40 pages of reading per week, and 50 percent did not take any course requiring more than 20 pages of writ-ing over the semester. The average student spent only

about 12 to 13 hours per week studying—about half the time a full-time college student in 1960 spent studying, according to the labor economists Philip S. Babcock and Mindy S. Marks.

Not surprisingly, a large number of the students showed no significant progress on tests of critical thinking, complex reasoning and writing that were administered when they began college and then again at the ends of their sophomore and senior years. If the test that we used, the Collegiate Learning Assessment, were scaled on a traditional 0-to-100 point range, 45 percent of the students would not have demonstrated gains of even one point over the first two years of college, and 36 percent would not have shown such gains over four years of college.

"We're Losing Our Minds"

Richard Keeling and Richard H. Hersh, in *We're Losing Our Minds: Rethinking American Higher Education*, make a similar point and call for a change in the entire academic culture. Specifically, as the authors told *Inside Higher Ed's* Doug Lederman and he reported in his February 9, 2012 piece, "We're Losing Our Minds":

No matter what the cost is, higher education is overpriced if it fails to deliver on its most basic promise: learning. Value is low when, as the research shows, too many of our college graduates are not prepared to think critically and creatively, speak and write clearly, solve problems, comprehend complex issues, accept responsibility and accountability, take the perspective of others, or meet the expectations of employers.

Keeling and Hersh make it clear that they seek a change in the academic culture, the reward system for faculty, and the allocation of institutional resources so that the emphasis for faculty is on effective teaching and student learning rather than on scholarship, research, and publication.

Is College Worth It?

William Bennett and David Wilezol promote their book *Is College Worth It?* with this statement on the book's cover: "A Former United States Secretary of Education and a Liberal Arts Graduate Expose the Broken Promise of Higher Education."

Bennett's critique is a harsh one. He argues that "two-thirds of people who go to four-year colleges right out of high school should do something else" and that "with new technology and online breakthroughs, [students] could get a better education in a coffee shop or [their] parents' basement" than at most colleges. He further writes: "In today's colleges, much of what is taught in the humanities or social sciences is nonsense (or nonsense on stilts), politically tendentious, and worth little in the marketplace and for the enrichment of . . . mind or soul."

A Williams College graduate with a PhD in philosophy from the University of Texas-Austin and a law degree from Harvard, Bennett does believe that there are 150 colleges and universities out of the country's 3,500 institutions that are worth attending. He has two criteria for judging. The institution is either one of the most highly ranked or offers a specialized field that is in demand, such as the Colorado School of Mines and Harvey Mudd.

The Economic Value of College and Postgraduate Degrees

Despite these criticisms, there is no question college graduates benefit significantly in economic ways. For example, the US Census Bureau, in "Work-Life Earning by Field of Degree and Occupation for People with a Bachelor's Degree: 2011," reported that college graduates on average earn $2.4 million over their lifetime, a million dollars more than those who do not graduate from college. Those who earn a doctorate increase their lifetime earnings on average by another million dollars.

The Value of a College Degree Beyond Financial Benefits

Moreover, several recent studies have demonstrated that a college education does have additional value beyond economic gain. After surveying graduates of four-year colleges, the Pew Research Center, in its May 15, 2012 piece, "Is College Worth It? College Presidents, Public Assess Value, Quality and Mission of Higher Education," noted, for example, that "74% [of surveyed graduates] say their college education was very useful in helping them grow intellectually; 69% say it was very useful in helping them grow and mature as a person; and 55% say it was very useful in helping them prepare for a job or career." The Pew report also stated that "college graduates place more emphasis on intellectual growth; those who are not college graduates place more emphasis on career preparation."

The College Board, looking at a wide range of aspects of the lives of those they surveyed, also concluded in its report, "Education Pays 2012: The Benefits of Higher Education for Society," that a college education provided great benefits beyond economic ones:

Adults with higher levels of education are more likely to engage in organized volunteer work and to vote. They are also more likely to live healthy lifestyles. The issue is not just that they earn more and have better access to health care; college-educated adults smoke less, exercise more, are more likely to breast-feed their babies, and have lower obesity rates. These differences not only affect the lifestyles and life expectancies of individuals but also reduce medical costs for society as a whole. Of particular significance, children of adults with higher levels of education have higher cognitive skills and engage in more educational activities than other children. In other words, participation in postsecondary education improves the quality of civil society.

Elected Officials Seek to Influence Higher Education

The governance of public institutions has a level of complexity that is not in the mix for private colleges and universities: that is, that in recent years some governors and state legislatures have sought to influence at a micro level certain institutional policies and practices as well as the specifics of the curriculum. Again, as noted in chapter 1, institutional policies have traditionally been the province of the board on the recommendation of the president and institutional practices the province of the administration. The curriculum and methods of teaching, of course, have traditionally been the primary responsibility of the faculty.

Today, however, ample numbers of public officials are advocating for a significant change in how education is to be "delivered." For example, some governors and members of Congress favor a shift to online courses and MOOCs instead of conventional classrooms. Several governors have also denigrated particular disciplines, particularly in the social sciences and the humanities.

There are of course plentiful examples of elected officials historically tying their position on funding for public campuses to political issues. Perhaps the most notable example involved Ronald Reagan's attacks on the University of California and his firing UC chancellor Clark Kerr in the third week of Reagan's governorship. A centerpiece of Reagan's gubernatorial campaign had been his attack on student protesters and his argument that Kerr and the faculty were too permissive in their response to those student protests. Reagan's attacks on certain departments (philosophy and sociology) had nothing to do with those disciplines per se but rather with his often-proclaimed complaint that they were "hotbeds" of radicals.

Today's attacks on higher education have contributed to several changes in how governance is being practiced on both public and private college campuses. Specifically, these attacks have impacted colleges and universities in the following ways:

- These criticisms have often put pressure on presidents to justify the value of the education that their institutions offer students and, in some instances, as has been the case with the University of Texas president William Powers Jr., to justify their leadership generally.

- These criticisms have attracted a new level of attention to the nature and value of the curriculum, leading some governors and other elected officials to interject themselves into the governance of colleges and universities in unprecedented ways, sometimes excluding faculty altogether from the decision-making process.

- These attacks have inspired some state legislatures to seek to mandate new academic requirements, specifically that the colleges and universities in their states give credit for completion of MOOCs developed by private vendors, again either without the involvement of the faculty at the credit-granting institutions or despite their objections. Efforts to pass such legislation in Florida and California were either defeated or watered down because of the objections of significant numbers of faculty members and administrators.

- These criticisms have similarly influenced trustees. As I will discuss in more detail in chapter 7, Christensen and Eyring's *The Innovative University* prompted the board leadership at the University of Virginia to seek to terminate President Terry Sullivan, in part on the ground that she was not moving quickly enough to embrace MOOCs.

- Attacks may have motivated some members of Congress to legislate some new criteria for federal research funding, limiting some of the social sciences from such funding.

- Criticisms have fueled the efforts of governors, state legislatures, and some boards of trustees to act on the notion that—despite evidence to the contrary—technology will be the panacea for higher education, providing a high-quality education at low cost.

Congress has also interjected itself into the decision-making process for federal research funding, which also has an impact on higher education.

Gubernatorial Efforts to Influence the Curriculum

Governors like Florida's Rick Scott, Wisconsin's Scott Walker, North Carolina's Patrick McCrory, and Texas's Rick Perry quite explicitly view higher education in utilitarian terms—that is, in terms of its value in preparing graduates for immediate jobs. Although it has long been the case that public institutions have often considered the employment needs of their states in terms of the programs that the institutions offer, what is new is that these governors and others quite publicly favor funding practical and technical courses at the expense of the liberal arts.

• Florida governor Rick Scott constituted a commission that recommended that students at Florida public institutions pay higher tuition for courses in areas not leading directly to jobs that the commission judged that Florida needs. Under this scheme, humanities, social studies, and art majors would pay more than students going into STEM disciplines.

In an October 1, 2010 interview with the *Sarasota Herald Tribune* editorial board, Scott also publicly denigrated the value of the liberal arts, citing anthropology as an especially useless major (even though his daughter was an anthropology major at William & Mary). Scott declared:

> We don't need a lot more anthropologists in the state. It's a great degree if people want to get it, but we don't need them here. I want to spend our dollars giving people science, technology, engineering, and math degrees. That's what our kids need to focus all their time and attention on, those types of degrees, so when they get out of school, they can get a job.

• Scott Walker of Wisconsin attempted—through the mechanism of legislative funding—to influence the nature of the programs that the University of Wisconsin system offers. In a November 16, 2012 speech at the Ronald Reagan Presidential Library and Foundation, Walker announced:

> We're going to tie our funding in our technical colleges and our University of Wisconsin System into performance and say, if you want money, we need you to perform. In higher education, that means not only degrees, but are young people getting degrees in jobs that are open and needed today—not just the jobs that the universities want to give us, or degrees that people want to give us.

• North Carolina governor Patrick McCrory on Bill Bennett's January 29, 2013 radio show echoed Scott and Walker by developing legislation that would award money to public universities and community colleges not in terms of enrollment, as is currently the case, but the success of graduates in securing jobs. He told Bennett that his approach is "not based on butts in seats but on how many of those butts can get jobs." Bennett and McCrory also questioned the value of philosophy and gender studies. Bennett, despite his PhD in philosophy from the University of Texas-Austin, asked, "How many PhDs in philosophy do I need to subsidize?" McCrory commented about gender studies, "If you want to take gender studies that's fine, go to a private school and take it. But I don't want to subsidize that if that's not going to get someone a job."

• Texas governor Rick Perry has openly challenged University of Texas president William Powers Jr. over the mission of the university and the level of tuition it charges. Specifically, Perry has publicly opposed raising tuition, something that Powers has advocated. Perry has also encouraged Texas public institutions to offer bachelor's programs that charge less than

$10,000 and to evaluate faculty based on student evaluations and the revenue that their courses yield.

Hunter Rawlings, president of the Association of American Universities, in an October 2012 speech at the University of Virginia, characterized the situation this way:

> Governor Rick Perry has, with the help of the Texas Public Policy Foundation, launched an assault on Texas A&M and the University of Texas, Austin: he wants an undergraduate degree to cost $10,000, and no more; he wants graduates ready-made for jobs; he wants faculty members evaluated on the basis of how much money they bring in and how many students they teach. . . . This is essentially to treat research universities as vocational schools, diploma mills, and grant-getters.

When faculty, staff, students, alumni, and members of the state legislature learned about the rumors that Powers might be fired by the regents, all appointed by Perry, they went public with their support. For example, within fewer than two days, more than 11,000 people had signed a Facebook petition of support for Powers. The state legislature then attempted to rein in the regents, passing S.B. 15 by a large margin. Perry has subsequently vetoed that bill.

Gubernatorial Efforts to Influence Tuition Policies

These governors, along with others, have called for constraints on tuition increases. For example, Virginia governor Bob McDonnell has called for tuition increases at a level no greater than the level of the consumer price index. Michigan governor Rick Snyder threatened public universities with the withdrawal of state funding if they failed to keep annual tuition increases under 5 percent. California governor Jerry Brown unsuccessfully favored a plan that would make some state funding for public universities dependent on the universities increasing the number of transfer students from community colleges by 10 percent, with these transfer students earning degrees within two years; the plan also called for tuition and fees at the public universities to be frozen for four years.

The level of tuition that an institution can charge, as I discussed earlier, inevitably affects the nature and quality of the academic programs and also how decisions are made.

Elected Officials Usurp Faculty Role and Award Credit for MOOCs

A number of elected officials have also embraced MOOCs and online learning, arguing that they will provide the antidote to rising costs and to the phenomenon on many public campuses that access to necessary courses is limited, thereby delaying or harming student graduation rates. For example, both California and Wisconsin have passed laws relaxing the requirements for MOOCs receiving credit toward graduation from the state's public institutions. In both instances, particularly in California, faculty mounted fierce opposition to the notion.

California S.B. 520

The California State Senate, for example, usurped the role of the faculty in establishing curriculum and academic standards when it passed S.B. 520. In brief, despite fierce faculty opposition, the California State Senate in April 2013 passed S.B. 520, which "would require state colleges and universities to grant credit to students who, unable to register for core classes at their home universities due to 'bottleneck' conditions at the entry level, opt to register for massive open online courses (MOOCs) instead." Private vendors could create the MOOCs.

The Senate took this action despite vehement opposition from faculty members, administrators, and unions. Specifically, the Senate received a letter outlining opposition from the University of California Faculty Senate, a petition signed by 1,600 Berkeley faculty members, and a letter representing the views of "the faculty, staff and labor organizations of the University of California (UC), California State University (CSU) and California Community Colleges (CCC) representing the 145 public higher education institutions in California."

The California Assembly is considering the bill. The protests continue.

Florida

In 2011, Florida passed a law mandating at least one online course for all Florida high school graduates. In 2012, Florida opened up the granting of credits at Florida institutions to out-of-state private vendors, despite concerns expressed both by the faculty and the Florida Virtual School, which already was offering online courses. The Florida legislature also passed and the governor signed a bill authorizing the University of Florida to develop a four-year totally online program.

Public Officials Seek to Influence Accrediting Agencies

Beginning with George W. Bush's education secretary, Margaret Spelling, public officials have begun to question the authority and value of accrediting agencies, which embrace the notion of peer review and which have great significance because institutions must be accredited if their students are to receive federal financial aid. Senator Lamar Alexander, himself a former secretary of education, pushed back against Spelling's efforts to add significant new regulations for the accrediting agencies, which pretty much nullified Spelling's efforts.

In recent years members of Congress have pushed for the accrediting agencies to have more flexible criteria when it comes to MOOCs, competency-based learning, and other innovative initiatives. President Obama in February 2013 called on the accreditors to include the criteria of price and value in their evaluations and to focus more on "performance and results."

Eric Kelderman, writing about this issue in a June 13, 2013 *Chronicle of Higher Education* article, "U.S. House Panel Questions Value of Accreditation," reported:

Republican members [of Congress] generally think accreditation costs too much for institutions, stifles innovation, and is too secretive. Democrats generally think accreditation goes too easy on for-profit institutions and doesn't safeguard parents and students from programs that will saddle them with debt and worthless degrees.

Clearly, a shift away from the current system of peer review to greater government involvement would constitute a major shift in governance in terms of how colleges and universities function and are assessed.

Congressional Efforts to Influence Research Topics

Normally, the federal agencies that provide support for research that often is conducted at colleges and universities, such as the National Science Foundation (NSF), the National Institutes of Health (NIH), the National Endowment for the Humanities (NEH), the National Endowment for the Arts (NEA), and the Centers for Disease Control and Prevention, have based their funding decisions on a fairly elaborate system of peer review.

However, members of Congress have for years attempted to influence what qualifies for research funding in some politically charged areas. For example, in 1996 the National Rifle Association (NRA) successfully lobbied Congress to prohibit the Centers for Disease Control and Prevention from funding any research related to gun violence.

More recently, in March 2013, in an unprecedented interference in NSF guidelines, the Senate voted to bar the use of NSF funds "for political science research not deemed essential to national security or economic interest." After the House of

Representatives accepted the Senate position, President Obama signed the bill into law on March 26, 2013.

Although Congress has made no effort to prevent faculty members from conducting research on topics some in Congress opposed, the constraint on federal funding for these topics has certainly prevented some scholars from being able to move forward.

Trustees Are Assuming More Activist Roles

American Council of Trustees and Alumni

The American Council of Trustees and Alumni (ACTA), an organization founded in 1995 by Lynn Cheney, former chairman of the National Endowment for the Humanities, encourages trustees and alumni to take a more activist role in all matters of institutional importance — including, in a more hands-on way than has historically been true of trustees, academic standards and the curriculum. For example, ACTA's "What Will They Learn" project rates approximately 1,100 American colleges and universities in terms of how many of what ACTA considers core subjects are taught. ACTA also actively encourages trustees to learn whether there is grade inflation on their campuses and if so suggests actions that trustees can take to address the issue.

ACTA has also embraced some of the recent works most critical of American higher education. For example, both Clayton Christensen and Bill Bennett, author of a recent book, *Is College Worth It?*, were originally on the ACTA board. The ACTA website cites Christensen and also Richard Arum and Josipa Roksa, authors of *Academically Adrift: Limited Learning on College Campuses*, as experts who inform its National Council.

In its 2009 guide *The Problem of Grade Inflation and What Trustees Can Do*, ACTA, after reminding trustees that they have ultimate responsibility for the institutions they serve, calls them to action: "Addressing grade inflation is one way to ensure the academic quality of your institution and to guarantee that students really get something for the tuition they pay. A strong stand against grade inflation serves your students and strengthens your school." ACTA does, however, acknowledge that grading is a faculty responsibility and so ultimately recommends that trustees ask for data and engage the faculty in a conversation about the negative effect of grade inflation.

ACTA does not share the reluctance of AGB to engage in political and partisan issues. For instance, ACTA's director, Ann Neel, weighed in on the dispute between the regents of the University of Texas-Austin, all appointees of Governor Rick Perry, with the University of Texas president and the state legislature. ACTA, which is apparently close to Virginia governor McDonnell, was one of the few higher education organizations, if not the only one, to endorse the action of the University of Virginia board to terminate President Sullivan.

The next three chapters will offer some cautionary tales about presidents, faculty members, and boards who either fail to fulfill their governing responsibilities or actively seek to undermine shared governance, followed by recommendations for what each of these groups can and should do to foster collaboration.

5

Cautionary Tales: Protests of Presidential Actions and Lessons for Shared Governance

Although campuses often experience conflicts over governance, the major points of contention more often than not occur when a substantial portion of the faculty believes that the institution's president has made decisions about what these faculty members believe to be academic matters without involving them adequately in the decision-making process. As this chapter will describe, there are also ample examples of presidents who have made decisions with only minimal consultation with the faculty and sometimes unilaterally, with no consultation whatsoever. These are the presidents who most often inspire faculty dissent and even votes of no confidence.

On some campuses, conflicts arise over the pace of change. Although presidents like the University of Virginia's Teresa Sullivan believe that the best decisions in the academy are made incrementally, other presidents—often at the directive of their boards—believe that change needs to be made quickly and all at once.

These conflicts become the most intense when the president and the trustees do not give great deference to the faculty on all things academic. And in fact, it is no longer the case that academic programs are viewed either as being sacrosanct or as being susceptible to change only with the concurrence of the faculty. It is no longer the case that academic programs and faculty positions are protected when it comes to cost cutting. Or to put it another way, although colleges and universities have often throughout their history made decisions in nonacademic areas prompted by scarce resources, the concerns about resources in recent years have led presidents and boards at a number of institutions, even those among the more affluent, to make decisions about academic matters based mainly on financial considerations.

Chief Financial Officers Seek Academic Cost Reductions

The 2012 *Inside Higher Ed* survey of chief financial officers (CFOs) at both public and private institutions affirms that many of those overseeing the budgets of their institution now look to the academic program for cost reductions. As several CFOs have explained it to me, in their institutions, the academic program is often the only area left where savings might be had.

The survey yielded the following results: 43 percent of business officers said their institution should be considering teaching loads even though it was not doing so. Forty-one percent wanted there to be some consideration of underperforming academic programs, and 41 percent said they would like tenure policies to be revised.

Other business officers reported more success in these areas, with 51 percent of respondents saying that eliminating underperforming academic programs was under discussion on their campus. Numbers were relatively consistent across sectors and institution types, meaning that tackling that issue might have more to do with institutional culture than with institution type.

In responding to the survey a year later, the business officers expressed a good deal of pessimism about the future of higher education. Only 27 percent had confidence in the viability over the coming five years of their institution's financial model. Half that number, 13 percent, had confidence in their financial model if they were looking ten years out.

Although the majority (57 percent) of the CFOs in the 2013 survey believed that they would need to reallocate resources within their institution rather than to count on new revenues, slightly fewer than half as many as the previous year (21 percent versus 43 percent) identified increasing teaching loads as a promising cost-cutting strategy. In 2013, the CFOs surveyed did not include "eliminating underperforming academic programs" in their list of top five cost-cutting strategies even though, in 2012, 42 percent thought that strategy "should be on the table." Fifty-eight percent now believed that developing and expanding online programs would produce new revenues for them.

I can only wonder whether the conflicts that have been occasioned when institutions have tried to make changes in the academic program have discouraged some presidents and financial officers from attempting to make changes on their own campuses.

This year's survey of chief financial officers was notable in another way. Ninety-two percent of the business officers now are focused on "retaining current students" as a revenue-producing strategy, seeing this as far more fruitful than "expanding online programs." Yet, as I argued in chapter 3, the increasing reliance of college campuses on contingent faculty, the majority of whom are part-time, through no fault of the adjuncts often runs counter to this desire for improved retention.

Faculty Votes of No Confidence in the President

Although to my knowledge, no one has tracked the number of faculty votes of no confidence in the president, it appears that such votes are happening more often than in the past. Often these votes are in protest of what faculty members judge to be a failure on the part of the president to honor the practices of shared governance when it comes to academic matters. In such situations, in addition to protesting what they see as unilateral decision making, faculty members also typically cite a failure of consultation or a process of apparent consultation that in reality either limits or ignores faculty input, flawed communication, and a lack of transparency on the part of the administration in academic and nonacademic areas alike. It is not uncommon for faculty members in such situations to criticize the emergence on their campus of what they see as a culture that is top-down and corporate rather than collaborative in nature.

Presidents and other members of the administration particularly come under attack when they do one or more of the following:

- Move too quickly in the view of the faculty and thereby violate the faculty's penchant for extended deliberations

- Eliminate academic programs that would once have been considered sacred

- Introduce new academic programs without faculty involvement

- Change how the academic programs are organized

- Alter how funds for departmental budgets and faculty lines are allocated

- Redefine the criteria for tenure and promotion

- Seek to create greater efficiencies and increase faculty "productivity" as defined by the number of students taught, class hours taught, or both

In my experience, most faculty members are reluctant to vote no confidence in their president. In many of the instances I cite, faculty members had concerns for an extended period of time. Thus, although I am sure that there are exceptions to what I'm about to say, it is my sense that the cause of faculty discontent generally is not a single presidential action or statement but rather an accumulation of actions or assertions that suggested presidential disregard of or disrespect for the faculty. The catalyst for a formal vote of no confidence frequently is simply the equivalent of a lit match being tossed into an already smoldering bush.

Moreover, not all votes of no confidence in a president are warranted or even caused by presidential action. For example, faculty members on some campuses have sought to undermine a president, who by most accounts had been effective, for reasons of personal animus, political differences, or simply an antipathy to anyone in authority. In addition, some faculty members have simply been unwilling to compromise; have been unwilling to let go of past grievances; have genuinely misunderstood the various responsibilities of the board, the president, and the faculty; or have been overly zealous in their expectations about the role faculty members should play in decision making of all sorts.

The examples that follow are not meant to be critical of any particular institution or president but rather seek to describe the kinds of significant problems that a failure of shared governance can create on college and university campuses. In this chapter and subsequent chapters, I will focus on and also name institutions whose stories have been widely reported in the press. In this chapter and in subsequent chapters, in order to preserve confidentiality for those colleges and universities that have been fortunate enough to avoid public attention and as I explained in the preface, I will try to disguise the identities of both the institution and the people involved. Sometimes I will change the location of the institution; sometimes I will assign the president, the board chair, or a faculty leader a different gender; and sometimes I will describe similar events that took place on more than one campus as though they had occurred at the same institution.

Highly publicized cases in the past few years at private universities like Gustavus Adolphus, St. Louis University, New York University, and Emory University and at public universities such as Florida Atlantic, SUNY-Albany, Marshall University, and Kean all illustrate the impact that contentiousness over who has responsibility for academic and related matters can have on an institution's students, its alumni, its faculty, and often its reputation. Many of these cases also indicate the way that faculty, students, and sometimes alumni have turned coverage of their protests in the local and national press and via social media into a powerful weapon.

Gustavus Adolphus

The ongoing conflict about governance between Gustavus Adolphus president Jack Ohle, who enjoyed the public support of his board during his six-year tenure, and the Gustavus faculty and the students is a particularly interesting case study because of the way that the students created and maintained a website to garner attention and support for their efforts to oust Ohle. Specifically, the website, www.gustieleaks.com, made available, not only to the campus and alumni of this Evangelical Lutheran college of approximately 2,500 students in St. Peter, Minnesota, but also to the general public, a running commentary complete with an array of documents pertaining to Ohle's leadership and to faculty and student discontent. Although the board and administration from time to time attempted to provide a counter-narrative, most of their efforts were soon criticized on the website. For example, the site contains a February 2013 letter from Mark Bernhardson, the chair of the board of trustees, to parents and friends expressing support for Ohle. That was immediately followed by a letter to the same group from the faculty senate, denouncing Ohle. Other primary documents include letters from Ohle to the faculty and faculty letters to Ohle and to the board. Some documents are newspaper accounts, including pieces from the student newspaper. Yet others are narratives written by interested parties. The site also contains the results of an annual survey of faculty opinion.

Ohle's problems reportedly began early in his tenure in 2008–09 when the provost, then at the beginning of her second year, resigned, according to multiple press accounts because

Ohle had reduced her responsibilities. Two months later, the two academic deans also resigned, citing lack of presidential support. The vice president for student life then accepted a position at another institution. At the end of the academic year, the faculty asked the board of trustees to review Ohle's performance, a request that the board denied.

Over the next several years, the relationship between Ohle and the faculty became even more contentious. In October 2012, the faculty voted 88–7 with 14 abstentions to ask the board not to renew Ohle's contract and to end his presidency as soon as possible. The board did not do so. A faculty group outlining what it called *A Narrative Guide* for the GustieLeaks website explained that its concerns about Ohle fell into three categories: "1) decisions that deprioritize the academic program, 2) unilateral and uninformed decision-making, 3) disregard for the traditions, values, policies, and mission of Gustavus."

The faculty had a long list of complaints. They argued that President Ohle ignored the faculty's primary responsibility for hiring their colleagues and that he made statements that he later contradicted. They criticized what they saw as a lack of transparency. They argued that the faculty did not have an appropriate role in the budget process. They were particularly angered that Ohle decided without consultation with the faculty to change the accounting system so that departmental funds would not roll over at the end of the year. Although most institutions that I know do not in fact roll over unspent funds and although that decision would generally be viewed as an administrative not an academic matter, Ohle's decision represented a change in practice that had a direct impact on academic departments. Gustavus faculty members were also critical that they were not given what they judged to be ample time to review and respond to changes in the board's by-laws, particularly those that referred to the *Faculty Manual*. Faculty members argued that there was no way for the faculty to communicate directly with the trustees.

Throughout, the trustees expressed support for Ohle. For example, in the February 3, 2013 letter to Gustavus alumni, the board chair on behalf of the board wrote:

> While we know there is work to be done, we are excited about the progress under the President's leadership. Be assured that the Board and President Ohle are committed to continuing to work with all of the College's stakeholders.
>
> Our alma mater has experienced significant success over the past few years. The College has realized an increase in student enrollment as well as significant increases in both the number of applicants and the academic quality of those applicants. In addition, thanks to the support of so many of you, there has been a substantial increase in giving to the College, including . . . the kick-off of a $150 million comprehensive fundraising campaign of which over $100 million has already been raised.

That same month, Ohle and the board laid out for the campus an eight-step program to try to address campus concerns, including bringing in an external reviewer to assess Ohle's performance, allocating $500,000 for each of two years to the academic programs to compensate for the funds transferred from departments in the accounting shift, arranging for direct interactions between the faculty and the board, and initiating listening sessions that Ohle would conduct with faculty, staff, and students. In other words, the president and the board tried to address the faculty's expressed concerns about both style and substance and to reassure them about shared governance.

Jack Ohle announced in May 2013 his plans to retire at the end of his current contract in June 2014, citing timing and his years of serving higher education. The board chair praised Ohle for presiding "over an ambitious agenda established by the Board," noting particularly successes in strategic planning, fundraising, alumni relations, the college's relationship with Sweden, capital projects, and enrollment. The board also noted that Ohle had created six new endowed faculty chairs and established a Center for Servant Leadership.

No one but Jack Ohle and perhaps members of the board know what prompted his decision to retire. What is clear is that the ongoing matter of the conflict between the campus and the president was serving as an unhealthy distraction for the institution.

New York University

Members of the New York University (NYU) faculty have for years objected to President John Sexton's NYU 2031 plan to add six million square feet to the campus in Manhattan, in Brooklyn, and perhaps on Governor's Island.

Although at most institutions, decisions about facilities would be within the purview of the administration and board, the situation at NYU was complicated by the fact that the university owns and rents to faculty, at a subsidized rate, 2,100 apartments in the Washington Square neighborhood. Professor Jeff Goodwin described faculty sentiment as he saw it in a March 20, 2013 op-ed piece for the *New York Times*, "The War in Washington Square":

> Dr. Sexton has consistently refused to address concerns about plans to expand N.Y.U. offices and dorms into the part of Greenwich Village south of Manhattan's Washington Square Park, where many of us live.
>
> This expansion plan is known as N.Y.U. 2031, indicating the year in which all the building will be complete. The very name told us that we'd be living on a construction site for a couple of decades.
>
> Not surprisingly, this did not go over very well with many faculty members. We were also concerned about where the money would come from to pay for this expansion, as no business plan for the project has been made public.

Many members of the faculty also objected to the Global Network University that NYU has established during Sexton's tenure by opening campuses in Abu Dhabi, Tel Aviv, Accra, Berlin, Buenos Aires, Florence, London, Madrid, Paris, Prague, and Shanghai. Opponents of the Global Network University argued that the motivation for it was financial, not academic, and that the various campuses were established without faculty approval. Goodwin also noted that many faculty members object to locating these new campuses in "countries where academic freedom, and free speech generally, are so parlous."

The NYU faculty also has been critical of Sexton's $1.4 million salary in 2012–13 and the $2.5 million bonus he will be given if he stays through 2015. Faculty members are equally unhappy about what they see as excessive compensation for other senior administrators, including a generous severance package for one of the senior administrators who reported directly to Sexton.

Although President Sexton has raised more than $3 billion and added 121 new faculty lines to the College of Arts and Sciences, the Arts and Sciences faculty in March 2013 voted no confidence in him. The faculty in the Steinhardt School of Culture, Education, and Human Development; the Tisch Asia Program; and the Gallatin School of Individualized Study followed suit, as did the Union of Clerical, Administrative and Technical Staff. The Gallatin faculty explained their vote this way:

[The university's] path of expansion has sacrificed academic integrity by devaluing faculty oversight and fair employment conditions for all faculty, has sacrificed student diversity by choosing growth rather than increased financial aid, and has sacrificed good citizenship by foregoing collaborative relations with both faculty and neighbors. The fundamental reason that the university has been able to take this direction, we believe, is that a top-down management structure and style discounted the voice of the faculty in setting priorities and making decisions. A lack of transparency in decision-making, and a failure to communicate, has compounded this fundamental problem of governance, and the result is an alienated faculty, large sectors of which are angry and demoralized. Rather than a community jointly engaged in resolving differences constructively, the university's leadership has produced polarization and rancor.

NYU faculty members have also held protests in Washington Square, enlisted celebrity support, and published a book, *While We Were Sleeping: NYU and the Destruction of New York.*

In contrast, the NYU board has been steadfast in its support of Sexton. For example, following the vote of no confidence from the Arts and Science faculty, the NYU board released a statement of resounding praise for Sexton's leadership that concluded with the following resolution:

> We, the Board of Trustees, endorse the strategic direction of New York University and John Sexton's stewardship. The transformation of NYU from a strong regional university into a university that stands shoulder-to-shoulder with the world's most revered universities is a remarkable accomplishment that is a testament to the dedication of the deans and the faculty under the outstanding leadership of John Sexton.

Later, in response to the vote of the Gallatin School, board of trustees chair Martin Lipton, again expressing "full confidence" in Sexton and outlining Sexton's accomplishments, said:

> We want the faculty of the Gallatin School, which has just completed its vote, to know why we view John's leadership with such confidence. Since John became President of NYU in 2002, the University has thrived

by almost any measure. Undergraduate applications are up 45 percent, freshman SAT scores have climbed, and financial aid has increased by 134%. NYU has moved upwards in national and international rankings, faculty recruitment and retention have been strong and successful, and initiatives have been started in new fields of study. The university's finances are stronger, fundraising has set records, long-range planning has been set in place, and important new investments have been made in academic facilities. And, uniquely among its peers, NYU has been redefining what a university is through the creation of its global network, which has allowed for unprecedented new educational and academic activities around the world for students and faculty alike.

For his part, in a May 2, 2013 letter to the faculty, Sexton noted the votes of several groups supporting him as well as those voting no confidence. He described his visits to various schools in an effort to listen and to answer questions. He acknowledged that under his leadership, NYU had "undertaken a lot of new, innovative initiatives in a short period of time, and regardless of how positive they are or prove to be, there could have been better communication and faculty involvement in them." Sexton ended his brief letter by saying that whatever the outcome of some remaining votes of no confidence, "I look forward to continuing to work together."

During the spring of 2013, a group of board members held a series of meetings with faculty and staff members, administrators and students. On August 14, 2013, the NYU board announced in a university-wide e-mail that John Sexton would retire in 2016 at the end of his contract. The board also announced that it would include faculty on the next presidential search committee; would create a new committee composed of trustees, administrators, and students and designed to improve communications between the faculty and the board; and would end an unpopular program that provided university loans for secondary residences. Board chair Martin Lipton explained the latter move to the *New York Times* this way: "This is a matter of extreme importance to us. . . . No university can prosper if there's disruption, if there's unhappiness in the family." Lipton further noted that a lack of faculty morale might negatively affect the university's credit rating.

St. Louis University

In August 2012, St. Louis University (SLU) provost Manoj Patankar proposed that all tenured faculty members undergo a review every three years. The faculty saw such reviews as being the equivalent to eliminating tenure. Although Patankar eventually withdrew the proposal, the SLU faculty senate in October 2012 voted no confidence in Patankar and in longtime president Father Lawrence Biondi. Students joined the protest through an array of events, including a "march to the Board of Trustees," which they announced on a Facebook page, "SLU Students for No Confidence." Patankar resigned in December.

Biondi is credited during his twenty-five-year tenure with, like Sexton, having transformed the university he led in positive ways. For example, during the Biondi presidency, SLU doubled the size of the student body and that of the campus. Father Biondi also received praise for contributing to the revitalization of the neighborhood around the campus and dramatically improving the university's financial situation.

Even after Patankar's resignation, the faculty and students continued to call for Biondi's resignation. For example, the faculty presented the board with a sixteen-page report arguing that the president should be fired for "unprofessional conduct," "failure to adequately support academics," and "mishandling of university finances." Specifically, the faculty accused Biondi of not appropriately involving faculty members in decisions to restructure the

College of Education and Public Service and to close the graduate school. The student protests continued.

The board next created its own problems with the campus. After a meeting at which the board and faculty leaders agreed to greater cooperation and communication, the faculty became disenchanted that the board had not acted in good faith. Specifically, a trustee leaked to the student protestors a memo the board chair sent to the trustees announcing that the board had retained a crisis communications firm to deal with the conflict. Of as much concern to the campus, in this memo the board chair both called for unanimous support of Father Biondi and also asked board members to refrain from talking with either faculty members or the media. Many members of the faculty were angered by the memo.

In May 2013 Father Biondi announced that he would retire but would remain in office until the board appointed a new president.

Emory University

Emory may be the most prominent example of an institution that has eliminated academic programs that once would have been considered central to its mission. Despite Emory's endowment of $5.36 billion, which most institutions would envy, Dean of the College Robin Foreman—reportedly without consultation with the faculty—in September 2012 announced to the faculty that Emory was closing its Division of Educational Studies, its Department of Physical Education, its Department of Visual Arts, and its journalism program. Foreman also announced that Emory would downsize the Institute of Liberal Arts and would suspend its graduate programs in economics and Spanish. The university would offer positions elsewhere at the institution to eighteen tenured faculty members, not renew contracts for three untenured assistant professors and nineteen lecturers, and eliminate approximately twenty staff positions over the next five years.

Although Emory is experiencing a budgetary deficit, Dean Foreman asserted that these changes were not prompted by the deficit but rather that they were designed to free resources to improve academic excellence by reallocating resources to new initiatives and areas of strength.

Although faculty and students vigorously protested both the decision and the process, in April 2013 the faculty of the College of Arts and Sciences rejected a vote of no confidence in Emory's president, James W. Wagner. The trigger for the vote was reportedly the president's unfortunate statement in the university's alumni magazine that the so-called three-fifths compromise "in which Northern and Southern politicians creating the U.S. Constitution agreed to count each slave in the South as three-fifths of a person for purposes of taxation and Congressional representation" was a model for compromise. But it was also the case that many in the minority that voted no confidence were deeply unhappy about the decision that the Emory administration had made to close the academic programs noted earlier and the way that the administration had come to the decision to do so.

Marshall University

Faced with a reduction in state support, Marshall University's president, Stephen Kopp, directed that all money in departmental accounts be moved into a centralized account. The impact of the decision was that departments could no longer carry funds over into the next fiscal year. The faculty protested that they had not been consulted. Although Kopp rescinded the decision, the Marshall faculty nevertheless in May 2013 voted no confidence. The board immediately reaffirmed its support for Kopp's leadership but encouraged him to work with the faculty to restore trust. Specifically, the board's statement read:

> Dr. Kopp has succeeded in achieving the goals set by the Board of Governors for Marshall University and he has exceeded the board's performance expectations in numerous areas. The board also believes that he is the right person to keep our great university moving in the right direction.

The university then created an ad hoc committee of members of the campus community to work with the administration to achieve a balanced budget, which the board has now approved. Although the faculty representative on the committee praised the process, he has also called for a permanent budget working group and more transparency going forward.

Some faculty members have taken the conflict to another level: the same week that the budget was approved, the American Federation of Teachers and two Marshall faculty members sued the university, seeking more detailed information about the budget and particularly about departmental budgets. Although private universities are required to make public their audited financial statements, they are not required to make available departmental budgets. The press coverage of this conflict has been extensive.

Florida Atlantic University

A series of events over a fourteen-month period, some of the administration's making and some the result of sheer bad luck, plagued the 40,000-student institution Florida Atlantic University (FAU), whose main campus is in Boca Raton, Florida. During this time, members of the faculty and students conducted a series of public protests and social media campaigns designed to oust President Mary Jane Saunders. Saunders's opponents claimed that she was high-handed, made academic decisions without faculty participation, did not support academic freedom, showed disregard for students, and harmed the institution's reputation. The board originally supported Saunders, but a crescendo of unpopular events and persistent press coverage led the trustees, all appointed by the governor, in an open session to question her leadership in April 2013 and Saunders a week later to resign her presidency.

The key events and the protests they inspired are described here.

In March 2012, the Florida legislature cut $24.5 million out of the Florida Atlantic University budget. The provost created a website on which faculty could post suggestions about where to cut.

President Saunders then constituted an administrative task force to make the decisions, which included among other things closing two satellite campuses and eliminating more than 1,000 summer school courses, one-third of the total previously offered. The decision was made solely on the numbers: all undergraduate summer school courses were eliminated that in the previous year had enrolled fewer than 24 students, and all graduate summer school courses were eliminated that had enrolled fewer than 12 students.

The faculty and students held public protests, noting that some of the eliminated lab and studio courses required low enrollments and that others were mandated by accreditation agencies. An online petition opposing the cuts attracted 750 signatures. Students mounted a Facebook page (https://www.facebook.com /SAVEFAUFTL) protesting the cuts. The president of the faculty union argued that the university was "using a top-down, one-size-fits-all approach to summer cuts" and did not take into account student needs or the advice of the faculty. Nevertheless, FAU closed the satellite campuses and restored only a few of the summer school courses.

In February 2013, FAU accepted a naming gift of $6 million for its new stadium from the GEO Group, to be paid over twelve years. Although decisions about naming gifts are traditionally matters for the governing board, campus groups at FAU protested the gift because GEO, which owns privatized prisons, had come under attack for mistreating prisoners. At an open meeting, the president and FAU board chair Anthony Barbar defended the gift, with Saunders calling it "a done deal." The Fort Lauderdale *Sun Sentinel* and the *Palm Beach Post* both covered the story in great detail, running pieces critical of Saunders. Students created a Twitter hashtag that played on the fact that the university mascot is an owl: #StopOwlcatraz.

The situation escalated to a new level when Saunders fled a group of student protestors on the Jupiter campus who wanted to talk with her about the gift. Saunders was taken by six campus security officers to her car, with the students in pursuit. As the president sped away, the side view mirror of her car hit the arm of one of the students, leaving a visible bruise.

The event led to more headlines. FAU's handling of the story in fact kept it alive. For example, when Saunders and Barbar said publicly that they thought the protesting students owed Saunders an apology, the press wrote about that. When the dean of students at the Jupiter campus then announced he was investigating the actions of the students who had made a statement to the police after the episode for possible violations of the student code of conduct, the American Civil Liberties Union weighed in, defending the students, who by now were being called "the Jupiter 7," and charging the university with intimidating them and retaliating against them for their complaint against the president. Again there was extensive press coverage, as there was when the university ended its investigation, with the associate vice president and dean of students writing the students, "while the University will not be initiating any disciplinary proceedings as a result of this incident, we hope that you can appreciate the impact that the incident had on President Saunders." The student who was hit by Saunders's mirror then publicly announced that she planned to sue Saunders. Her father then issued a statement to the press calling for President Saunders to apologize to his daughter.

During this period, FAU also received national press attention because FAU communications professor James Tracy suggested in January 2013 that the massacre at Sandy Hook "never took place—at least in the way law enforcement authorities and the nation's news media have described it" and then in April raised doubts about the reliability of press accounts of the shootings at the Boston Marathon. Because Tracy posted his comments on a personal blog and not the university's website, FAU did not take disciplinary action against him but did denounce his statements.

In March 2013, FAU instructor Dr. Deandre Poole attracted national criticism from some national political and religious leaders after one of his students complained to the press that Poole had asked students to write the name Jesus on a sheet of paper and then step on it. The purpose of the exercise, which had been used in communications courses for decades, was to show the power of language, and indeed most students immediately refused to step on the paper. FAU issued a statement denouncing the exercise, apologizing to those who were offended, declaring that the exercise would never again be used on campus, and putting Poole on administrative leave, asking him to stay away from the campus for reasons of his safety.

The FAU faculty senate criticized Saunders for not defending academic freedom, for making decisions about Poole without consulting with faculty members who might have helped explain the context of the exercise, and for promising that the exercise would not be used again.

By now, Saunders had no reservoir of goodwill. Police were reportedly stationed both in and outside her office. She was accompanied on campus by a bodyguard. Battered by the press coverage, GEO withdrew the gift. The FAU trustees in an open meeting chastised Saunders for the administration's failure to handle effectively what had become public relations problems. Scott Travis, in an April 16, 2013 *Sun-Sentinel* (Fort Lauderdale, Florida) piece, "FAU Trustees Criticize President's Handling of Incidents" described the events this way: "Florida Atlantic University's poor handling of recent events has threatened campus safety, hurt the school's image and resulted in the loss of a $6 million gift, members of the Board of Trustees said on Tuesday."

In the aftermath of board meeting, President Saunders resigned, citing the press coverage as one of the reasons. Her statement read:

> The issues and the fiercely negative media coverage have forced me to reassess my position as the president of FAU. I must make choices that are the best for the university, me and my family. My hope is that in

the future, news stories and public discussions about FAU will return to the accomplishments of our faculty, students and staff across all of our campuses.

Because Florida's sunshine laws keep little private, the announcement of Saunders's resignation was immediately followed by stories about how for the next several years she would serve as a tenured professor in the College of Science at a salary of $276,000 (80 percent of her base presidential salary of $345,000). Her responsibility will be to assess the feasibility of developing a physician's assistant program at FAU.

Soon after Saunders's resignation, FAU's provost and others in academic affairs also resigned. The university rehired Deandre Poole for next year and has begun a national search for a new president.

The State University of New York at Albany

In October 2010, the State University of New York at Albany (SUNY-Albany) administration announced, without extensive consultation with the faculty, that it was phasing out language programs in French, Italian, Russian, and classics as well as the theatre department. The only foreign language that the university planned to offer going forward was Spanish. As Scott Jaschik noted in his October 4, 2010 *Inside Higher Ed* piece, "Disappearing Languages at Albany," "the language decision runs counter to the university's motto: 'the world within reach'." The university also indicated it was cutting in half the number of journalism courses and transferring the one remaining faculty member in Judaic studies to the history department.

As Jaschik also reported, Albany president George M. Philip attributed the cuts to the fact that state funds to administrative units on the campus had been cut by 22.4 percent and to the academic programs by 16 percent. He noted that the state legislature refused to give the campus authority over tuition and to release the institution from costly regulatory requirements. He further argued that the decision had been "based on an extensive consultative process" and low enrollments in the affected programs.

The response to these cuts was immediate and fulsome. There were protests from the faculty, students, and alumni. Members of the foreign language departments at Stanford wrote Philip to suggest the importance of foreign languages and alternatives to the decision. Eventually, the university decided to retain French, Russian, and theatre as minors rather than majors, something that did not go far enough to please those protesting the decision.

Kean University

In the spring of 2010, also citing financial problems because of reduced appropriations from the state of New Jersey, Kean University reorganized the academic programs but without the involvement of those academic programs. Specifically, Kean dissolved its academic departments and eliminated the position of department chair in favor of schools with executive directors appointed by the president. The Kean faculty and staff vehemently opposed the plan, which the board nevertheless approved. The university had previously eliminated the departments of philosophy and social work, and other departments such as graphic communications and educational psychology were slated for elimination because of low enrollments.

Members of the Kean campus community have since then protested this and other actions, calling for the firing of the Kean president, Dawood Farahi. For example, students have organized "Occupy Kean," a group that has organized protests on campus, including a student "walkout" from class. The board has been steadfast in support of Farahi, even when it became public that he had falsified his resume.

Recommendations for Presidents

Trustees, senior administrators, faculty, and staff, to varying degrees depending on the circumstances, all have critical roles to play in the functioning of a college or university. Nevertheless, my experience tells me that presidents more than anyone else determine the nature of and pace of change on a campus.

It is also clear to me that the pressures on and expectations for presidents in recent years have expanded significantly. At the same time, presidents need to continue to fulfill all the traditional responsibilities of their position. As a result, the sheer scope of presidential responsibilities is daunting.

Although good presidents have always navigated well the new challenges their institutions are facing, today these challenges are often unusually complicated. For example, presidents now need to address the rising protests against ever-increased tuition at a time when many institutions are experiencing diminished resources. Presidents need to understand and provide leadership on the use of new technologies for teaching and learning. Some need to provide leadership in determining how best to educate new nontraditional populations of students. Presidents often need to identify and then establish new revenue streams. Many need to deal with public officials and their local community. But most of all, presidents need to bring about change in ways that satisfy their boards and, at the very least, gain the understanding and acceptance of their faculty colleagues and in some circumstances the students, the staff, the alumni, the community, and elected officials.

At the same time, presidents need to fulfill a wide array of more traditional responsibilities. A president needs to develop a strategic vision for the campus that is grounded in the institution's mission, that is informed by data and financially sound, and that has been developed collaboratively with the campus, the board, alumni, prospective donors, and sometimes the local community. To be successful, presidents must inspire these same constituencies to embrace the vision and the goals that derive from it. Presidents need to provide leadership to their senior administrative team and essentially direct and oversee the institution's operations. Presidents are charged with recommending policies, the operating budget, the institution's strategic priorities, and tenure and promotion decisions to the board. A president needs to raise money (preferably lots of it) and be an articulate spokesperson for the institution both internally and externally. Good presidents also encourage creativity and foster teamwork.

What follows are some specific recommendations for presidents that will, I hope, enable them in positive ways to influence the tone and the nature of discourse on each campus about governance and the level of collaboration and communication among the various constituents, including students, alumni, elected officials, and the local community as well. In chapter 8, I will offer some specific examples of presidents who have been successful in these ways.

Recommendation 1: Presidents Need to Listen Throughout Their Tenure

During presidential searches, I am pretty confident, most candidates describe their intention to spend a good part of their first year on campus listening to all the constituencies and learning about the campus and its strengths, challenges, and opportunities. The best presidents, I believe, in fact spend time this way not only in their first year but also actively throughout their presidencies. The best presidents also take into account what they've heard and acknowledge when they've been influenced by their conversations with members of the campus community.

Recommendation 2: Presidents Need to Encourage Dissent and Be Open to Other Views

College and university presidents often have an enormous amount of power or at least are perceived to have that power. That power derives from a number of factors. Members of the senior administration typically serve at their pleasure. Members of the faculty generally need a positive recommendation from the president for tenure and promotion. Presidents also ultimately control how resources on their campuses are allocated, including funding for programs and faculty lines, equipment, and facilities. I remember once asking a president who served on the university's space committee. He pounded his fist on the table and then smiled at me as he said, "I am the space committee." And he was.

Because of the president's power (and often her or his prestige), members of the campus community frequently are hesitant to disagree with a presidential opinion or decision, at least openly. Effective presidents therefore proactively encourage dissent. They also take into account and address the arguments of their critics.

A very effective president I know had been encouraged by the members of his cabinet to make a decision that had to do with food on campus. The benefit of the decision was financial. The president announced the decision. The students reacted negatively. Some student leaders wrote the president, expressing why they opposed the decision. The president found their argument compelling and so wrote an e-mail to the campus, announcing that he was reversing the decision based on persuasive arguments from students. By doing so, he made it clear to the entire campus that he was interested in and willing to learn from alternative points of view. He also earned great respect for admitting that he had made a mistake.

Recommendation 3: Presidents Need to Understand "the Vision Thing"

As I noted earlier, the best presidents, after taking account what they have learned from and about the campus, develop and articulate an inspiring vision for the institution going forward. They are also responsible for ensuring that all constituencies understand both that vision and the institution's mission.

The University of St. Joseph

The University of St. Joseph (USJ or St. Joe's, formerly St. Joseph College) in West Hartford, Connecticut, for example, recently introduced a new doctoral pharmacy program. Located in attractive space in downtown Hartford, the three-year program for its first class enrolled 67 students, for its second class 80 students, and for its third class 90 students. The program is on track going forward to enroll 100 students for each class. All students are full-payers. The tuition is almost $40,000 per year. The students come from all over the country.

The story is one of presidential vision, a sense of urgency on the campus to address significant enrollment and budgetary problems, and a willingness on the part of the faculty to collaborate.

Pamela T. Reid became president of the University of St. Joseph in January 2008. The university, which defines itself as being "enhanced by the Catholic intellectual tradition and the values of its founding Sisters of Mercy," is a woman's college for undergraduates and an institution that serves men and women completing bachelor's degrees in its program for adult learners and in its graduate and continuing education programs.

The university website provides the following information about Reid's background:

> Pam Reid holds a B.S. from Howard University, an M.A. from Temple University and a Ph.D. from the University of Pennsylvania. She has more than three decades of faculty experience in psychology, education, and women's studies at diverse institutions, and has held administrative roles at the City University of New York Graduate School, the University of Michigan, and Roosevelt.

Almost immediately Reid recognized the possibilities for a doctoral program in pharmacy. She first tested the ideas with several highly respected faculty members, including a retired and highly respected faculty member, a nun who had been a professor of chemistry. Those with whom she consulted liked the idea. She then discussed it with her cabinet, which similarly encouraged her to move forward. Finally, she met with the faculty and staff in a community meeting to lay out her ideas for the institution.

She told her new colleagues that although conventional wisdom had it that "new Presidents shouldn't have new ideas for nine months, I'm from New York and I listen really fast."

Reid made a presentation that focused first on St. Joe's current situation. She described the institution's mission, emphasizing that community service was part of St. Joe's mission and integral to a number of its majors. She noted St. Joe's historical strength in the sciences, especially in biology and chemistry, both of which had already created online programs. She talked about the institution's strong reputation in counseling, nursing, and nutrition. She discussed the importance of building on the college's strengths and taking advantage of its standing in the health care community and its relationships with area hospitals. She also shared national reports on the need for pharmacists and explained that the only pharmacy school in the state was at the University of Connecticut and that regionally there were only a few private universities in Massachusetts that offered a pharmacy program.

The group achieved consensus that the institution should move forward with the pharmacy program. Reid then commissioned a feasibility study at the request of the board, a study that a trustee funded. She talked to the president at a competitor institution, explaining that St. Joe's would be offering a different model. She learned that there was support within the local community and decided to rent space in downtown Hartford for the program.

Although many on campus were concerned that the institution was going to have to invest resources in establishing the program by hiring faculty, purchasing equipment, and renovating space, Reid argued that over time there would be a large return on these investments. The graduate council approved the program.

The faculty also endorsed introducing off-site graduate classes in education throughout the state, tripling the size of the graduate program in education. The undergraduate enrollment has also grown.

Carroll College

Carroll College's new president, Thomas Evans, similarly gave the lie to the notion that every president needs to wait a year to articulate a vision. During the search process, the search committee of this Catholic college in Helena, Montana, was clear that it wanted to hire a president who could articulate an inspiring vision for the college going forward and then mobilize the campus and trustees to act on it. The search prospectus put it this way:

> Carroll is looking to its next president to articulate a vision for advancing the College based on conversations with the campus community and the board about Carroll's strategic imperatives, as well as a thorough assessment of the College's strengths, weaknesses, opportunities and challenges. The president will also bring a set of experiences and market perspectives that will help to inform analyses of strategic alternatives and environmental scans and benchmarking about what is happening at peer and aspirant institutions.

Evans previously had been the associate vice president for professional education and global initiatives at St. Edward's University in Austin, Texas. He majored in Japanese and minored in theology at Georgetown University and earned a master's degree in Asian studies and a doctorate in educational administration from the University of Texas-Austin.

From the time he was appointed president in December 2011 and took office in June 2012, Evans spent as much time as he could on the Carroll campus, listening to everyone with whom he met. Everyone with whom he talked said that they were eager to hear his vision for the future. At a summer faculty retreat, the refrain was that the faculty was tired of talking and of planning that resulted in no action. The faculty simply wanted "to get on with it."

By the end of the summer, Evans recognized that there was a great deal of agreement on the campus about what was important and what was not. After the faculty retreat, he crafted a several-page paper outlining his own thoughts about where the college should go. He discussed this draft first with the faculty, then with the staff, and then with the students, generating lots of enthusiasm. In the fall, he laid out for the board this vision that had quickly earned the support of the campus. The trustees enthusiastically endorsed this approach.

Recommendation 4: Presidents Should Be Transparent and Clear

To the extent possible, presidents should communicate honestly and fully with the campus about the decisions that they are making and the reasons for those decisions. The exceptions of course are personnel matters and matters that really do require privacy. But even in these cases, presidents can try to explain what privacy laws and institutional policies mandate.

In one particularly contentious personnel decision involving a popular member of the student affairs staff who had been let go for cause, the student body president alerted the president that the student senate was about to censure her for the decision. The president asked if the student body officers could meet with her, the dean of students, and the college attorney first. They agreed. They all gathered later that day at the president's on-campus residence for several hours. Over refreshments, the attorney answered all of the students' excellent questions about privacy laws and confidentiality related to personnel matters. These students came to understand why the administration could not explain what had happened. The students that evening shared what they had learned with the student senate and recommended against a censure vote. The senate agreed. Not only was a crisis averted, but also from that point on the student leaders and members of the administration actively sought to resolve problems in a collaborative manner.

There are also times when a president may need the support of his or her board. In one such case, a president had let go a very popular faculty member, again for cause. Not only were some students distraught, a number of parents became involved. Eventually, the board chair and president agreed that the board chair needed to address the issue with the angry parents. He did so by writing a brief letter explaining that although he, like the president, was not at liberty to disclose the details of what was a confidential matter, he did want these parents to know that prior to acting in this matter, the president had consulted with the appropriate board committee, which had strongly endorsed the president's proposed action. That letter may not have made the parents happy, but it did stop them from continuing to berate the president.

I also know of several presidents who worry that although they strive to communicate fully and frequently, their messages are often ignored. One president, stung that the students accused him of a failure to communicate, met with the student government to discuss what he could do to communicate with them more effectively. The students were not able to help him, telling him that they didn't read e-mail coming from the university and resented text messages from the administration. (He did encourage them to read the texts, explaining that the administration only sent texts in the event of an emergency.) Few of them read the student newspaper. Few of them checked the university's Facebook page.

My advice here is to develop an internal communication strategy that employs as many approaches as possible. I also have come to believe that overcommunicating is far superior to communicating too little.

Recommendation 5: Presidents Need to Differentiate Between the Urgent and the Normal

Despite my comments throughout about the urgency of some matters, there are also many questions that come before the faculty that can rely on and even benefit from extended deliberation. Presidents thus would be wise to push for immediate action only when they deem it essential. They also need to explain to the faculty the reasons particular decisions do in fact require immediate action and the timetable by which decisions must be made and actions taken.

Recommendation 6: Presidents Need to Be Clear About Process, Responsibilities, and Financial Decisions

It is good practice for presidents, as they introduce a subject for faculty consideration, to be clear about the process that will be followed, including how they intend to involve the faculty in the decision. As significantly, presidents need to clarify who will have responsibility for the decision and the ensuing actions. I suggest that they do so in meetings with the faculty and also in writing.

For example, if presidents are announcing a search for a new vice president, they would be wise to clarify how members of the committee will be selected and to emphasize that the committee's role is advisory to the president rather than being a decision-making one. If presidents want to discuss with the faculty a policy that they will recommend to the board for its action, they need to explain to the faculty that they want to understand faculty perspectives on the matter before coming to a recommendation, which the board might or might not accept. Finally, presidents need to communicate the financial elements of decisions, including why the decisions need to be made, where—if appropriate—the resources to fund these decisions will come from, and the probable financial implications of those decisions.

A Personal Example

At the beginning of my second year at Puget Sound, I began what became an annual "fall faculty conversation" in which the faculty and I met for four hours (with appropriate breaks for food) to discuss matters of institutional importance. These were not formal faculty meetings, so no votes were taken, nor did we use *Robert's Rules of Order*. Rather we talked. At this particular gathering,

I shared with my colleagues what they had consistently told me were two of their major concerns when I met with each department throughout my first year. They had explained that because we had a bimodal distribution of students, it was hard to know how to pitch their classes. Second, faculty members feared that they were ignoring the better-prepared and more-motivated students in order to reach the students who were not well prepared or motivated. Faculty members believed that as a result a disproportionate number of our most academically talented students were transferring because they were bored.

In light of these observations, I asked a member of the staff to analyze the pertinent data. His report proved that the faculty was right on both counts. We did have a bimodal distribution of students, and a disproportionate number of our better students were transferring. We also looked at the experience of what we thought of in shorthand as "the last hundred students we would have admitted" (based on a formula of SAT scores and grades). These students, it turned out, accounted for one-third of all disciplinary problems in the institution, and one-third of them had left the university by the end of their first year, mainly for either disciplinary or academic reasons. We did a similar analysis for transfer students and learned that a disproportionate number of those students were leaving because of academic difficulties. We concluded that we had been admitting students who were not capable of doing the work and that admitting them (with many of them taking out loans) was unfair to them.

In the interest of addressing this situation, I told the faculty I was contemplating recommending to the board that we reduce the size of the first-year class from 700 to 650 and transfers from 160 to 80. I noted that we had not once in ten years met the goal of enrolling 700 students. I also laid out the budgetary implications of this reduction in the size of the student body in the interest of quality and fairness. I said at the outset that this was not a matter on which faculty members had a vote, but that I very much wanted to know what they thought.

We talked about this for several hours. The group came to an almost unanimous consensus that we should go forward. We did so. The results fairly quickly were better than even I had hoped in terms of student quality. Retention also improved significantly.

Had I unilaterally made this recommendation to the board without either the analysis or the consultation with the faculty, I am confident that there would have been an outcry. Instead, the faculty was invested in the decision and also came up with a series of new and creative programs that I'll describe in the following paragraphs.

Recommendation 7: Presidents Need to Encourage Creativity and Innovation

This particular decision about enrollment at Puget Sound had another unanticipated consequence. Prompted by the focus on retention, a number of my colleagues came up with new programs intended to retain more students, including those who were high achievers. For example, the chair of romance languages established a very successful language house in which majors lived together. Other faculty members agreed to teach first-year seminars for students who lived in the same section of a residence hall, adding an array of cocurricular experiences to the class (such as going to movies or concerts together). Several faculty members agreed to take on the project of advising especially promising students as early as their first year about what they needed to do to be competitive for graduate school and for such fellowships as Fulbrights, Watsons, and Goldwaters (and our numbers soared). New interdisciplinary courses and programs blossomed.

Recommendation 8: Presidents Should Serve as Models for Their Campuses

Effective presidents create a context that fosters not only creativity but also collaboration and communication. They model institutional thinking and require their senior staff to do the same. In many ways, they are teachers, explaining to all constituencies where their institution fits within the landscape of higher education and how all constituencies must commit to the health and well-being of the entire institution and not just to their own program or set of interests.

Recommendation 9: Presidents Must Exhibit Integrity and Seek to Engender Trust

Exemplary presidents don't compromise doing what they believe is right in order to curry favor with others. These presidents develop reputations for being truth tellers rather than people who cater to their audience. They seek respect, not popularity.

Although many contentious moments about governance on college campuses, like those described earlier in this chapter, tend to be precipitated by presidential actions or management style, it is also the case that members of the faculty can provoke and, in some instances, can resolve the problems. The next chapter will discuss examples of how faculty, for motives of their own, can shatter or advance shared governance.

6

Cautionary Tales: Faculty Failures and Recommendations for Collaboration

This chapter is meant to balance the litany of national press stories, described in chapter 5, about faculty who protested presidential actions that in their judgment violated faculty rights and responsibilities or at least faculty sensibilities.

The mini-case studies that I offer in this chapter illustrate that it is dangerous to generalize about the nature of faculty opposition to a president or to assume that all such actions are motivated by something the president has done or said. Rather, these examples suggest that some faculty members at some institutions contribute to or indeed create an adversarial relationship with the president for reasons of their own.

Although certainly there are other motivations for conflicts between the faculty and the administration, in my experience one or more of the following factors is typically at play:

- Faculty members are trained as teachers and scholars to be critical and independent thinkers and to be deliberative in their approach to teaching and scholarship. It is therefore not surprising that they approach institutional matters in the same manner.

- In contrast to some trustees and some presidents, most faculty members believe that the highly deliberative processes of shared governance ensure that their institution will be true to its mission, will preserve academic values, and will protect academic freedom. That faculty members mount protests against and even challenge the authority of presidents who, in their judgment, ignore the processes of shared governance, particularly in academic matters, is therefore predictable and understandable.

- Even in circumstances in which faculty members may acknowledge the need for more rapid decision making, in my experience the vast majority will resist any and all decisions that they regard as top-down. Again, they will vigorously seek to preserve what they believe to be their prerogatives and indeed their rights. When they have reason to believe that their president, board, or both are failing to fulfill their fiduciary responsibilities, faculty members are further inspired to what they see as necessary vigilance.

- Some faculty members challenge the authority of the president because they disagree with particular presidential actions and decisions.

- Some faculty members simply distrust either their current president or in fact all administrators and so oppose presidential decisions and actions on principle rather than because of any specific aspect of presidential performance.

- Some conflicts over governance have their roots in an institutional culture in which faculty members believe that they rather than the administration have authority over all matters that in any way touch on the education of their students.

- Some faculty members are unable to let go of some moment in their institution's history when it was ill served by a previous president and so see every current circumstance through the lens of that experience.

- Sometimes faculty members, for reasons of their own, seek to undermine their president. Although the final example in this chapter describes such a situation, it also illustrates how the deliberate efforts on the part of several respected senior faculty members can support a beleaguered president and change a potentially negative campus dynamic to a positive one.

As a number of cases described in the preceding chapter illustrate, even if the faculty, administration, and board at a particular institution have historically enjoyed mutual respect and have comported themselves with civility, when the president, who may or may not be new to the institution, makes decisions that in some ways ignores or even compromises shared governance, mutual respect is replaced with mistrust, and civility is abandoned.

Case Studies: Faculties That Resist Administrative Decisions

In the examples that follow, faculty members refused to cooperate with the administration in a variety of situations. Such resistance inevitably led either to overt conflict or to dysfunctional paralysis. Only one of these stories had a happy ending.

Course Scheduling and Academic Freedom

When I first became chair of the English department in my fourth year at Ithaca College, I rearranged the course schedule in order to give our students more choices. In so doing, I sought to honor as best I could the preferences of the faculty. Most people appreciated what I was trying to do and were accommodating to the new schedule.

In one instance, however, I shifted a senior professor's upper division course from 4 p.m. on Monday, Wednesday, and Friday to

3 p.m. I assumed that he would be pleased with the shift. Instead, he was enraged. When I told him that the schedule was set for the coming semester but that I would see what I could do in future semesters, he raged that I was denying him academic freedom. He made an appointment with the president to make the same claim. The president agreed with me that course scheduling was not a matter of academic freedom but an administrative responsibility of department chairs.

I remember being deeply puzzled by this professor's reaction until another member of the department explained to me that our colleague preferred scheduling his classes late in the day, especially on Friday, because few students chose to sign up for courses at that hour. His motive was to reduce the number of papers and exams he had to grade and the number of students with whom he might need to meet outside of class.

I was reminded of this story, which happened several decades ago, when I learned that the faculty of an institution in a metropolitan area with a great many commuter students protested vigorously the decision of a new president to schedule courses in ways that he too believed would serve students better. He was further motivated by a desire to use the physical plant more effectively.

For years, the campus had offered only a handful of Friday classes because faculty members increasingly wanted their Fridays free to write or consult. Some members of the faculty also argued that their commuter students preferred three-day weekends, which they further claimed made their students more competitive for weekend employment.

The effect on the campus of this four-day course schedule had over time been profound. Residential students, finding themselves with a three-day weekend, tended to leave the campus after their last classes on Thursday afternoon and to return to campus late on Sunday. The commuter students came to campus only for their classes and to meet with faculty during office hours. The company providing food service began to limit both the hours and the variety of food offered on Friday through Sunday, citing their limited clientele on those days. Eventually, the company limited food service on Sunday to midmorning brunch. The library soon closed at noon on Saturdays and didn't open until noon on Sunday. The numbers of students living on campus declined. Retention, always shaky, became even more of a problem.

The president first consulted with the student affairs staff, which explained that it was nearly impossible to create student activities on weekends because so few students were around. The staff shared with the president their worries about those students who did stay on campus over the weekend, reporting that many of them were lonely and that certainly some of them were spending time in their rooms alone, drinking excessively. As evidence, they described to the president the number of liquor bottles that the maintenance staff collected from the residence halls every Monday morning.

The president asked the staff to hold some focus groups with both commuter and residential students about this matter. The staff soon learned that most of those with whom they met preferred to have their classes spread out over five days. The current schedule, many students explained, meant that many of the courses that they needed to fulfill requirements were offered at the same time, thereby extending the amount of time it took them to graduate. An expanded schedule would, they believed, give them more options. Some commuter students said they'd like more classes in the evening. Some of the residential students confirmed the impression of the student affairs staff and said that being on campus over the extended weekend was pretty depressing. Most were critical of the limited amount of time food was unavailable and the limited menu of choices.

The president announced to the faculty that he had directed the provost going forward to craft a schedule in which one-fifth of all courses would be offered on Friday. He laid out the reasons in great detail. In so doing, he reminded the faculty that the board had been slated at its next meeting to receive a proposal for a new academic building that had been a priority of his predecessor but that the current president had decided that he could not in good conscience recommend, unless he could demonstrate that current facilities were being used effectively and that the university needed additional classroom space.

The faculty resisted the new course schedule. Some claimed that the president and provost were violating their academic freedom. The provost responded that course scheduling and decisions about facilities were not matters of academic freedom but were administrative prerogatives. She appealed to the faculty to put the needs of the students first. She asked them to recognize the cost to the institution of having the physical plant go unused three-sevenths of the time and the cost of having so many small classes.

The provost went ahead and scheduled Friday classes for the coming academic year. Some department chairs tried to schedule only classes taught by adjuncts on Friday, but most were unable to do so. The tensions over this matter spilled over into other areas of the institution. Some faculty members refused to serve on committees. Some came to campus only to teach their classes and hold office hours. Some shared their displeasure over the president's action with students.

Although the president expects that going forward there will be far more students on campus on Friday and although he has insisted that food be served more often and amply on Friday and over the weekend, the campus is far from being a happy place.

Faculty Members Refuse to Develop New Revenue Streams

Faced with a significant structural deficit, the board of a small private college directed the president to develop new revenue streams. The ensuing extensive and inclusive strategic planning process resulted in the recommendation that the faculty craft a handful of new master's programs in areas in which the college was already offering undergraduate degrees and therefore for which it already had expertise.

The president accepted the recommendations and asked the dean of the faculty to work with the recommended departments to create the new master's programs. At the same time, the president announced that the college would increase enrollments in its freshmen seminar program from thirteen to fifteen, would increase enrollments in its very popular theater program, and would offer classes with six or fewer students in alternate semesters rather than every semester.

The faculty, understandably distressed because they had gone several years without a raise, responded that they would refuse to develop the necessary new courses unless the pertinent faculty members were given release time and were paid stipends to do so. A number of faculty members also decided that they would no longer participate in activities designed to increase enrollment (such as presenting at admission events and calling prospective students) unless they were compensated for doing so. The president argued that such actions would harm the institution and promised that if the college were able to increase enrollments, the additional revenue would go to faculty and staff compensation. No one budged.

Three years later, the structural deficit was still significant. The faculty and staff still had been given no raises. Some trustees have begun to question the long-term viability of the institution.

A Faculty Votes Down Recommendations on Program Prioritization

Early in 2009, the effective decade-long president of a highly selective institution, confronted with some modest financial challenges she wanted to address immediately, established a program prioritization process. A committee composed of faculty members and the vice president for academic affairs spent the academic year analyzing course offerings and enrollment patterns. The committee ultimately recommended that the university phase out two majors and one minor that the committee judged were not central to the institution's mission and not financially sustainable. Each of these programs enrolled at the most only a handful of students, who were taught by an equivalent number of faculty members.

As part of the phaseout, the recommendation called for the tenured faculty to continue to teach at the college. After the majors and the minor were fully eliminated, these faculty members would have the option of teaching courses in other departments if those departments so approved or of teaching interdisciplinary courses in the freshmen and senior seminar programs. The untenured faculty would be retained only for the duration of their current contracts. Thus, although the savings would not be immediate, eliminating these programs would free up resources over time.

The college's by-laws required that any changes in the academic programs be approved by a majority of the faculty. The entire faculty spent the following year debating the committee's recommendations. Ultimately, faculty members voted overwhelmingly to keep the majors and the minor at their current level of staffing because they did not want to set the precedent that any major or any minor at all should be abolished.

The president was disappointed that the faculty would overrule one of its own committees but concluded that there was nothing more that could be done about the low-enrollment programs.

Department Chairs and Change

The board of a reasonably affluent undergraduate university of several thousand students hired a new president with a mandate to improve the quality of the academic programs and to clarify that the institution was now focused on the liberal arts rather than on the vocational programs it once had offered. The board chose someone who had previously been a chief academic officer at two institutions and had successfully championed similar efforts.

Over his first summer, the president and the provost met at the president's house for several hours over wine and cheese with each department, asking the faculty in those departments to explain to the president the strengths and challenges of their programs. At the end of that process, she decided that two key departments had more of a technical than a liberal arts focus. For example, the business department was offering undergraduates a sort of mini-MBA program for practitioners. The communications department was teaching students, as the president later explained it, how to point the camera but not how to think about the meaning and purpose of what was being filmed.

The president and the provost then met with each department to discuss the shift in approach that the president favored and that the provost supported. The president acknowledged that she could not "force" the departments to make such changes but said that she hoped that they would see the wisdom of doing so. She also offered each department stipends so that the faculty could work together over the summer to design the new curriculum.

The president made no effort to dictate the contents of such a curriculum but rather asked that the new majors focus on critical thinking and effective writing and argumentation rather than technical training. She offered the departments money to bring in consultants if they wished and to buy potential course materials. She said that she would fund two people in each program if they wished to visit other campuses with exemplary programs in these areas that had a liberal arts focus.

The business faculty immediately agreed to move forward that summer. The department had a number of impending retirements and agreed that this was an ideal time to reexamine the department's focus. The business faculty also had long felt themselves to be second-class at the institution and saw this effort as a way to improve their standing with their colleagues and also to attract what they came to think of as "more-better" students.

In contrast, the chair of the communications faculty, who had held that position for more than two decades, balked. (Although at some institutions, the faculty elects department chairs, at this university the president appointed chairs for indefinite terms on the recommendation of the provost, who first consulted with the faculty.) In front of his colleagues, the chair told the president that she was out of line and was violating the department's right to chart its own course. He insisted that the communications faculty would not accept the additional resources. Several of his colleagues interrupted what was becoming a tirade and told the president that the chair was not speaking for all of them. At that point, the president said that she wanted briefly to adjourn the meeting in order to speak privately with the chair in his office. She asked the others to please remain where they were and said that she would be back within ten minutes.

During the private meeting, the chair continued to rant at the president that she had no rights in this matter. The president remained calm but told the chair that, as was her prerogative under campus policies, she was launching a national search for a new chair that afternoon and was going immediately to appoint an interim chair. She encouraged the now former chair to return to the meeting with her and gave the chair the opportunity to say that he was resigning in protest at the new direction for the department. The former chair refused to rejoin the meeting and said that he wanted everyone to know that the president had fired him.

Returning to the department, the president learned that the department was split about revising the curriculum but that department members were for the most part pleased that they would have a new chair. The president said again that she could not of course force them change the curriculum but that she hoped that they would do so. She said that she would leave them to discuss the matter. Later that afternoon, they advised her that they would move forward with the revisions.

The former chair spent the remaining years of his career trying to stir up protests against the president. He wrote a letter to alumni to encourage a letter-writing campaign to the board, and he tried to motivate students to protest. He got no takers.

Within five years, both departments were pleased with the changes that they had made and particularly with the quality of the students they were attracting and the new faculty colleagues they were able to hire. The communications department was especially pleased with the chair it had chosen after a national search. The former chair eventually retired.

The Power of the Past

In *Requiem for a Nun*, William Faulkner wrote, "The past is never dead. It's not even past." I think of this quote when I encounter college and university faculty who are so firmly embedded in an unhappy institutional past that they find it impossible to imagine working collaboratively with their president and other senior administrators. Recently, I was on a campus where this phenomenon seemed especially pronounced.

The president, now in his fourth year, had earned the trust and respect of much of the campus. Since his first year, the university had been enjoying surpluses, something that had not occurred in the previous decade. He had also raised money, made positive changes in how the administration functioned, and given the faculty and staff raises after years of frozen salaries and diminished benefits. The college also had built a much-needed new residence hall and renovated two others, actions that appeared to have contributed to improved retention and admissions.

Nevertheless, the faculty complained a good deal about "the administration." One senior professor told me that the faculty had for a long time been left out of the budget process. Because I knew that the current president had established a budget process that gave a central role to members of the faculty, the student body, and the staff, I asked for an example. He shared with me several stories about events that had taken place during the tenure of the two previous presidents, one eight years ago and the other more than ten years ago. When I pointed out these facts and reminded him that his concerns about wanting a transparent inclusive budget process had been addressed, he responded that even as he knew that, it was essential that the faculty be vigilant because presidents by their nature could not be trusted. Other faculty members were still stung by a tenure decision that had occurred prior to the current president's tenure. Yet others complained that the faculty had too little contact with the trustees, even though this current president had added faculty representation to the board and to board committees and had significantly increased the opportunities for trustee-faculty interaction.

The president characterized the situation this way: "Lots of people, but thankfully not all, are still trying to slay dragons that became extinct at the end of the last administration." He reconciled himself, he said, to the fact that some members of the faculty would never be able to judge him for who he is and what he does.

Faculty Members Misunderstand Shared Governance

Faculty members at a small private university were pretty uniformly convinced that they "ran the college" and that the president's sole role was to raise money, meet with alumni, and make speeches.

In fact, this faculty did have unusual authority over many matters. For example, the committee that decided on which students to admit was composed not of members of the admissions staff but of members of the faculty, with the admissions staff providing them with support. A faculty committee, rather than the vice president for academic affairs, oversaw the allocation of positions that came open through retirements, resignations, or negative personnel decisions. The dean of students reported to the vice president for academic affairs rather than to the president and needed the approval of a faculty student life committee for any new programs or policies in the student life area. The faculty committee on athletics saw itself as overseeing all intervarsity and intramural sports.

This approach had become the norm at this university decades earlier when the institution had hired a president who preferred to make peace rather than hard decisions. Sensing an opportunity, the faculty had drafted a "constitution" for itself. This document outlined the faculty's elaborate committee structure and defined what it claimed was the faculty's authority in most areas of campus life. The document also included a number of other provisions that were outside the realm of the standard practice for shared governance. For instance, the document called for the faculty to recommend tenure and promotion directly to the board, leaving both the chief academic officer and the president out of the process. The document mandated that a "committee on faculty concerns" be formed and that this committee meet privately with the board for an hour at every meeting, so that the faculty could share their thoughts directly and, they hoped, confidentially with the trustees.

The president shared the document with the board, which decided that since the "constitution" conflicted with the university's governing documents, it had no standing. Acquiescing to the desire of the president to avoid conflict, the trustees accepted his recommendation to ignore the document. The dean and the president had always made recommendations to the board about tenure and promotion. They continued to do so in closed session but did not report this part of the process to the faculty. Because the dean and president in every instance had embraced the faculty's recommendations, the faculty assumed that their judgment was the prevailing one. The board also decided to meet with the faculty group without the president. The president told the board he had no problem with this approach since he was confident that the trustees would share with him what they learned. This decision, too, gave the faculty the impression that the board had approved the "constitution," but no one ever directly asked.

Because the vast majority of the faculty had taught only at this institution, they mistakenly believed that their practices were standard across higher education. They were startled when their acquiescent president retired and their new and promising president told them that she believed it essential that all institutional documents be consistent, clear, and reflective of best practices. She also wanted the faculty to understand their role, her role, and the role of the board, including tenure and promotion processes. Finally, she told the faculty that she did not object to faculty members meeting with the trustees but that she and the trustees were agreed that in the future she would be present at those meetings.

The president brought a consultant to campus for several days of meetings with the faculty to share with them all of the institution's governing documents, particularly the board's by-laws, which the faculty had not previously reviewed, as well as a sampling of faculty handbooks from a series of their peer and aspirant institutions.

In reading these documents, the faculty recognized that the board had ultimate legal authority for the institution and that, as was the case at most institutions, the board delegated the university's operations to the president. The faculty also learned that it was common practice across the country for the faculty to recommend tenure and promotion to the chief academic officer, who then recommended to the president, who in turn recommended to the board. The faculty came to understand that they had unusual access to trustees and that their private meetings with the trustees were far from standard practice. Some were dismayed, however, to learn that the "constitution" on which they had relied had no standing.

To their credit, most members of this particular faculty were interested in understanding what the national norms were. Because they had high hopes for their new president, they also wanted to demonstrate their desire to work closely with her. After the consultant advised them that a conflict over governance with the board would result only in problems that no one wanted, the faculty agreed to work with the president to resolve the questions of responsibility and authority.

The president and the dean over the coming year met regularly with the faculty group drafting the handbook. The faculty signed off on the new handbook, which the board approved. The new handbook did include the statement that the board's by-laws took precedence over the provisions of the faculty handbook and that the board had ultimate responsibility for all institutional policies and practices and the budget. Although a few members of the faculty objected to this phrase, the president informed them that the statement from the board's point of view was a "given" and therefore was nonnegotiable.

For her part, the president told the board that although the new handbook had resolved the key legal issues, there were still likely to be some struggles on campus over jurisdiction. To minimize those conflicts and even more because she decided that the various faculty committees had actually worked pretty well, she made no effort to change the nature of the committees, making it clear nevertheless that the faculty's role in these committees was advisory.

Shared Governance Within the Faculty

Questions of shared governance are not limited to the relationship of the board, the president, and the faculty. These questions also can come into play in terms of how faculty members interact with one another.

I have been fortunate to teach and be an administrator on campuses where senior faculty have taken very seriously their role both to mentor their junior colleagues and also to encourage those colleagues to take an active role in governance. These senior faculty have welcomed the perspectives of their newer colleagues.

Unfortunately, I have also observed campuses where a very different dynamic takes place. Several years ago, for instance, I was invited to give a lecture at a top-tier institution. At a dinner with a group of assistant professors, I learned that they did not believe that the administration would in any way compromise their academic freedom or their freedom to participate in governance. Rather, they told me, there were a group of senior faculty, whose support the assistant professors would need if they were to receive tenure, who sought to influence the assistant professors' and every untenured faculty member's stance on campus issues. Later, without naming those with whom I'd talked, I described the conversation to the provost, who immediately agreed that this was a problem that she had been unable to eliminate. More recently I learned about a situation on another campus, where a handful of senior faculty members who opposed the president had for all practical purposes "silenced" those of their junior colleagues who approved of the president.

I have also been on campuses where assistant professors do not speak in faculty meetings out of concern that they might alienate a senior colleague. On one such campus, because every tenured faculty member has the right to vote on every tenure decision in the college, their junior colleagues were concerned about winning the support of senior faculty not just in their own department or program but across the entire college.

Supportive Faculty Thwart Efforts to Undermine a President

In contrast to these unhappy stories, I also know of a case in which a group of faculty united in support of a president whom some of their colleagues were attacking. This president had been hired with the explicit charge of emphasizing the college's religious heritage and further institutionalizing its religious values. The faculty members and the student on the search committee appointed by the board chair had been selected because they agreed with these goals. The search prospectus informed potential candidates that the campus believed that a more deliberate identification with its founding denomination would better differentiate itself from its competitors and better engage its alumni. During a visit to campus as a finalist, the selected candidate heard this refrain from all quarters.

Literally within days of the new president's arrival on campus, before she had even finished setting up her office, she encountered resistance from a small but very vocal group of faculty members who declared her too conservative for their tastes. She found this surprising because in fact her policies were more consistent with the denomination's progressive wing. The president wondered privately whether their discontent with her appointment stemmed from the fact that she was a woman.

Although they had no examples to cite, her critics began to describe the president as being "holier than thou." They also began to spread untrue rumors about her. One such false rumor had it that she had ordered an array of books in the library to be burned. Another was that she planned to hire, tenure, and promote only faculty who shared the denomination's most conservative views, even though her record as a provost at a previous institution of the same denomination suggested that she had used no such litmus test and actually favored hiring faculty with a diversity of viewpoints. She also had a record of encouraging a campus climate in which students of all faiths and of no faith at all would be welcome.

This president was by all accounts respectful of the faculty and by nature consultative. She thus reached out to her detractors to try to achieve common ground. They refused to meet with her, telling her that they had nothing to talk about. Because she had within her first few months solicited and received a $5 million gift which she successfully encouraged the donor to dedicate to faculty development, to two new faculty lines, and to the academic programs generally, her detractors' complaints got little traction. She thought she had weathered what she described as being storm clouds rather than a full-blown storm.

Toward the end of her first year, however, she found herself confronted with a problem she had done nothing to create. A student group recognized and funded by the college had, at the suggestion of their faculty advisor, invited a controversial speaker to campus, someone of some note whose public disagreement with the denomination's stance on several social issues had attracted headlines. Some prominent leaders within the denomination publicly demanded that the president withdraw the invitation to the speaker. The faculty senate privately wrote her, asking her not to rescind the invitation, citing academic freedom. Privately, the president agreed with the faculty sentiment, but she worried about damaging her relationship with those religious leaders outside the campus.

Caught between the vehemence of those leaders who were demanding that she cancel the speech and the clear sentiment of the campus that she not do so, the president decided on what she thought of as a compromise: she invited a second speaker, who embraced the denomination's positions, to join the controversial speaker, turning the single presentation into a panel. The controversial speaker agreed to this approach. Many on the faculty and the involved students were mollified by this compromise. The president's original detractors were not.

The president then constituted an ad hoc committee, comprising two trustees, two senior administrators, the chair and vice chair of the faculty senate, and the president and vice president of the student body, to develop a speakers policy. The committee codified the president's approach—that is, that any speaker who did not share the denomination's views on matters of importance must be joined by a speaker who would advocate for those views. The board approved the policy.

The issue, however, remained alive. The book-burning rumors were revived. The admissions office worried that if the conflict became public, it might discourage some students from enrolling. The president decided that she needed the help of some of her faculty supporters. She called together half a dozen senior and highly respected faculty members and asked for them to intervene. Two of them sent a letter to the entire faculty, praising the president, outlining her accomplishments, and dismissing the complaints as false. All of them talked with colleagues about how damaging it would be for the college and for the capital campaign that was in the planning stages if the president were to leave. These efforts calmed what now was in danger of becoming a full-blown storm.

Five years later, the president is still in office. The disgruntled faculty members remain disgruntled but recognize that they have been marginalized. The institution by a great many measures is thriving.

Recommendations for Faculty Members

I am personally convinced that faculty members are the heart and soul of every good college and university. As I said earlier, in the acknowledgments, I have in my own career been able to count on the collective wisdom of the faculty. I am always inspired by the work that I see members of the faculty do at both healthy and dysfunctional institutions. Indeed, I am confident that even at those institutions where the faculty as a body has voted no confidence in the president, the vast majority of individual faculty members are teaching to the best of their ability and engaging in whatever level of scholarship is appropriate to that institution.

Even so, I am equally convinced that the faculty as a body as well as individual faculty members in today's environment must be willing to make decisions in a much more timely fashion than has traditionally been the case. In some instances, these decisions need to be made immediately. In other words, when colleges and universities are struggling as so many are today, faculty members no longer can take months and often years to debate issues that require urgent action.

In short, it is crucial that faculty members embrace new approaches to governance that focus on institutional health rather than primarily on faculty processes, faculty prerogatives, and the programs or interests of individual faculty members. Faculty members also need to be willing to collaborate with the board and the president and to abandon the position that trustees and administrators are the faculty's natural adversaries and are not to be trusted.

I recognize that my argument that members of the faculty need to think anew about governance may be controversial for many if not most members of the faculty. But even as I understand that,

I am absolutely convinced—as the early chapters of this book have demonstrated—that many boards and presidents are now minimizing and even ignoring altogether the notions of shared governance. I further believe that the contentiousness we are seeing across the country on so many college campuses is in great part a response to the fact that on many campuses, faculty members do in fact have a more minimal role in the governance of their institution than was the case a decade or more ago.

A friend of mine, after reading the opening chapters of this book, e-mailed the following response to what I had written, a response that I suspect others will share:

> Why are you admonishing faculty to relinquish some sort of shared governance, or at least find a new way to come to quicker decisions, or somehow streamline their process, when it is the administration that has gotten them into [economic difficulties] to begin with?

I answered my friend that I thought he was oversimplifying the causes of today's economic pressures and ignoring the importance of collaborative solutions to problems. I reminded him that there are many examples of presidents who have made an enormously positive difference at their institutions, differences that advanced teaching and learning and that clearly had the support of the faculty. But I also said what I believe to be the case: unless members of the faculty proactively seek to work collaboratively and, when circumstances call for it, expediently to address problems, they will become increasingly marginalized. Colleges and universities will continue to hire contingent faculty members. Boards will continue to press for entrepreneurial decisions and actions. And more and more presidents will come not from an academic background but either from a background outside the academy or from the areas of finance, development, enrollment, public relations, and occasionally student affairs.

To put it in clichéd terms, I fear that the train has already left the station. I am therefore persuaded that it would be far better for faculty members to be an active part of the conversations about governance and to become active partners with their presidents and boards going forward. If they don't, I expect that the metaphorical train will continue to increase its speed and pick up more and more passengers.

What I am going to advocate in this chapter seems obvious but clearly has been elusive on many campuses.

Recommendation 1: Faculty Members Need to Understand the Higher Education Landscape and Think Institutionally

It is commonplace on college campuses that faculty members identify with their department and their discipline rather than the institution. Faculty members tend to resist what they see as the corporate notion that they are employees. Nearly a century ago, the *1915 AAUP Declaration of Principles on Academic Freedom and Academic Tenure* made this point explicitly, arguing that even though faculty members are appointed by the board of trustees, they are not employees. Rather, the *1915 Declaration* insists that faculty owe their primary responsibility to the public and their profession. The statement ignores the fact that faculty members are also paid by the institution.

I am advocating a counter-viewpoint: that faculty members today need to recognize that if their college or university is to thrive, they need to make choices that will serve the best interests of the institution as a whole rather than merely their own particular interests. In order to do so, they need to be interested in where their institution is positioned within the higher education landscape in order to understand and respond productively to its challenges and opportunities.

Hendrix College, a small private college located just outside of Little Rock, Arkansas, in Conway, provides an example of how faculty and administrators working together, in a compressed period of time, transformed an institution that had unexpectedly found itself in jeopardy because of new external forces not of its own making. It is also an example of how members of the faculty came to understand that how the college positioned itself in the marketplace mattered and that the programs that the faculty members devised contributed to that positioning.

The oft-told story is instructive. In 2002 the Walton Foundation gave the University of Arkansas $300 million to expand its honors program and to support its graduate school. At the same time, the state of Arkansas cut scholarships that had previously supported in-state students choosing to study at Hendrix. The college understandably became deeply concerned about the impact of these events on enrollment.

The Hendrix faculty and administration worked together to create the Odyssey Program, which built on Hendrix's existing strengths and its focus on experiential learning. The faculty also understood that the college hoped the Odyssey Program would prove attractive enough to prospective students and their families that Hendrix could increase both its tuition and its financial aid discount. The result was a large increase in enrollment rather than a decline and an increase in net tuition revenue.

I am indebted to Bob Entzminger, Hendrix College provost, and Rock Jones, former executive vice president at Hendrix and now president of Ohio Wesleyan, for providing me with the following information.

In August 2003 then president Tim Cloyd proposed to the faculty at the Fall Faculty Conference a new program that would differentiate Hendrix from public university honors programs by highlighting the college's commitment to out-of-class learning, such as undergraduate research, study abroad, internships, and service learning. The board of trustees for its part embraced the idea and directed the administration to move forward with designing and implementing such a program.

Tom Goodwin, who had had just been named the 2003 Carnegie/CASE National Teacher of the Year for Baccalaureate Institutions, was asked to chair a task force that included other faculty members, staff members, and students. Bob Entzminger, as provost, served on the committee *ex officio*. The committee's charge was to develop a program for a faculty vote in April 2004. The committee struggled with the following three questions:

- Should the program be universal (in other words, required) or voluntary (that is, more like an Honors Program, which a consulting firm had originally recommended and which the faculty had rejected)? Some committee members were concerned that a requirement might deter students from attending Hendrix.

- What categories should be included, and how many should be required?

- How could the program be credentialed?

The task force met biweekly through the winter and early into the spring, hashing out these and other issues, and reporting to the faculty at their monthly meetings. Bob Entzminger reported that the question of whether to require the program was the most vexing. He noted, however:

The problem was resolved, brilliantly, when the students volunteered to poll the graduating seniors about their participation in such activities. They found that over 50% of the students had completed at least two of these experiences, over 75% at least one. This poll also served to reassure the faculty that they weren't being asked to take on a very large additional commitment. In effect, we found that we were already doing this; we just wanted to do it more intentionally and systematically, and provide for more support. . . . The program was re-named Odyssey.

In March 2004, the task force presented its recommendation to the faculty for discussion. In April, nearly 75 percent of the faculty voted to approve the program. In May, the trustees too accepted the task force's recommendation and directed the college to move forward with marketing and full implementation in time for the entering class of 2005. Hendrix did add staff and other resources to support the new required projects.

The trustees supported the program with gifts of their own, and eventually a significant portion of Hendrix's $100 million campaign that concluded in 2011 was devoted to support of this program. For instance, gifts endowed Odyssey experiences and established twelve Odyssey professorships, which rotate among faculty.

When Hendrix began the process of considering the Odyssey program, the college enrolled barely 1,000 students. Today, enrollment is more than 1,400, with an increase in geographic diversity. For example, in 2003, about 40 percent of Hendrix students came from outside Arkansas; today, about 55 percent are from out of state, and the international student population has grown dramatically, in large part due to study abroad initiatives originally funded by Odyssey.

Professor Goodwin, the chair of the task force that led to Odyssey, explained to Jack Stripling in an August 5, 2010 *Inside Higher Ed* piece, "Hendrix's Odyssey," that the faculty came to understand that their careers and the college's market position were intertwined. Specifically, he said, "We [faculty] like to think we're above all that stuff. We don't like to think of education as a business. It kind of taints what we're about. But unfortunately in the real world you have to pay the bills. In this economic climate, some colleges are going under."

Recommendation 2: Faculty Members Sometimes Need to Expedite Processes

The Hendrix and the University of St. Joe faculty both are examples of faculty members coming together to expedite processes.

Recommendation 3: Faculty Members Should Avoid Demonizing All Administrators

As I was writing this chapter, I coincidentally reconnected on Facebook with a former tenured member of the faculty at the University of Puget Sound, someone whom I confess I had not thought about in a decade.

In one of our exchanges, he apologized for having been a vehement critic of mine, which I then recalled that he had been. He reminded me of a meeting we had in my office early in my tenure, which in fact I don't remember. I am sure his version is accurate. He said that he and I had essentially agreed on a course of action that was designed to advance Puget Sound's mission as a liberal arts college, an action that I hoped the college would take and that we did eventually take. He explained that despite the fact that he agreed with me, he had felt the need to oppose whatever I was proposing because of what he called "politics." He added that during that time in his life he had been ornery (and probably still was). I responded that I appreciated being in touch with him again.

I tell this story because, sadly, it is not an unusual one, nor is it probably unique to college campuses: some people find it difficult for personal or political reasons to support the decisions and actions of those in leadership positions, even when they agree with them. In the case of my former colleague, as in many other similar cases, I also expect that the politics in question had little to do with the substance of the actions being considered or taken but rather that these actions would constitute change, something that in itself was unwanted.

I had a similar experience a few years ago with a student who wrote me to apologize for having said terrible things to and about me, prompted, he said, by the views of a faculty critic of mine. Now that he was more mature, he wrote, he recognized that he had been wrong both in his judgments and his behavior. Although I had no recollection at all of this particular student or of any student behaving terribly to me, I thanked him and said that his e-mail had brightened my day, which it did.

A former president recently told me a related story. He had heard from a faculty member for whom he had a great deal of respect and whom he had gotten to know well. Having just retired, the faculty member wrote that she was rethinking her career and wanted to apologize that she had not stood up to her more negative colleagues when they had demonized this president. She felt guilty that she had not been a more vocal supporter of his presidency, which she admired. He wrote her that he especially appreciated her note and was afraid that being demonized often came with the presidential territory.

Recommendation 4: Faculty Members Should Give Presidents the Benefit of Their Best Thinking

Several years ago, in my role as a consultant on a campus with a new president, I met with a number of faculty committees. In each instance, those with whom I met told me about their concerns about an international program that the previous president had established. These faculty members had reason to believe that the program had been losing a good deal of money and was of dubious academic quality. They also believed that the previous president and the chief financial officer had withheld that information from the board. These faculty members said that the previous president had curried favor with the board leadership by taking them on a visit to this international campus, on the college's dime.

When I asked if any of them had shared their understanding of the situation with the new president, each said no. When I asked why not, they answered that they did not think it appropriate that they be so candid with the president who, as one person put it, "is after all the president." Each group agreed that I would tell the president about their concerns. The faculty members also agreed to talk with the president about what they knew if he would like.

Although I am not encouraging members of the faculty to engage in end runs or to trade in gossip with the president. I am advocating that if they have knowledge of something that is harming or might harm the institution, it is their responsibility to bring it to the president's attention, perhaps, if appropriate, first working with their dean.

I know of a number of situations in which members of the faculty, unhappy with a presidential decision, have done just that and to good effect. In these instances, members of the faculty have met privately with the president and persuaded him or her to take a different course. They have done so out of a clear commitment to their institution and in a way that they hoped would solve rather than create problems.

A Search Committee Apologizes to a President

An especially interesting example of a faculty and president coming together in a newly collaborative fashion grew out of the hiring of a new provost. After a national search, the president and the search committee, composed of six faculty members, had agreed unanimously to bring two candidates to campus. The president favored the first candidate, with whom she had worked previously, but at the end of the campus visits, a fairly large number of faculty members strongly favored the second candidate. Their concern: they were afraid that the first candidate was too close to the president and so might not "stand up" to her but rather would, as one person insisted, "be in her pocket." These same faculty members also were concerned that the first candidate would not be an advocate for the faculty. The president shared her very different perspective: that this candidate, in their past working relationship when she had been a provost and he a dean, had indeed made clear to her when he thought she was making a mistake. This quality was one of the things she valued most about him.

Nevertheless, because the president agreed that the second candidate was a viable one, with excellent credentials, experiences, and recommendations, she accepted the search committee's recommendation and appointed him. She also had decided that it would be unfair to her former colleague to appoint him as the chief academic officer in the face of opposition from the faculty. She won points on campus for doing so. Her former colleague appreciated her candor.

Within weeks of the second candidate's arrival on campus as provost, the president had concerns. He seemed erratic. He did not use e-mail, despite the fact that he had presented himself as being a "tech whiz," a fact that also concerned the staff in information technology who reported to him. He chose to ignore the president's wishes on two matters that she deemed important, telling her later that he assumed she was only advising and not directing him.

The president struggled with how to handle the situation. She did not want to consult with faculty members about how this still relatively new provost was doing, because she didn't want to appear to undercut him. For all that she knew, he had the full support of the faculty. She decided to lay out her concerns and expectations in writing for the provost, and they met for several hours to discuss those concerns and expectations. A month went by, during which the provost did nothing to allay her worries and a fair amount to increase them.

At that point, the faculty members on the search committee asked to meet with her. They told her that they owed her an apology and that the provost had been the wrong choice. They recounted a series of unhappy stories about him. For example, he had not responded to requests for important information from department chairs. He had refused to meet with a group of senior faculty who had hoped to counsel him on how to work more effectively with them. He not only did not return e-mail messages, he also did not return phone calls.

The president had a heart-to-heart with the provost, and they came to an agreement that he would step down immediately and teach for two years until he retired. The president reconvened the search committee, which this time was particularly interested in her perspective.

A Department Chair Advises a President

A department chair shared with the dean of the faculty her worries that the president was isolating himself and in the process was alienating the faculty. The dean shared those concerns. With his encouragement, the chair decided to have what she thought of as an intervention with the president. She invited the president and the dean and their spouses to dinner at her home, hoping that this informal atmosphere would lead to a more comfortable and extended conversation than would be possible in a thirty-minute meeting in the president's office.

When she stopped by the president's office to extend the invitation, the president said that he would be delighted to attend and that he hoped it was OK if he came alone since his wife was out of town. He added that he was touched because this was the first time a member of the faculty had invited him to his or her home. They arranged the details. Then, as the department chair was leaving, the president called out to her, saying that he had a favor. He asked that she not include other members of the faculty in the dinner.

The dean's wife decided not to attend what was clearly a business meeting. During dinner, the chair explained to the president how his failure to interact with the faculty was leading to a good deal of mistrust and also uncertainty on the campus. She told him what she believed: that if he would share his vision and his ideas more transparently with the faculty, at least at talks at the beginning of the semester, he would inevitably garner more support. He agreed to do so. Although he never was able to socialize with the faculty, he at least became more accessible during working hours. He also on occasion reached out both to the chair and the dean for advice on matters of significance.

This chapter has focused mainly on the relationship of the faculty and the president. The next chapter's focus will be on the board of trustees. It will include some cautionary tales about boards that have failed to fulfill their fiduciary responsibilities and will make recommendations for how trustees can more effectively govern.

7

Cautionary Tales: Boards That Fail to Fulfill Their Fiduciary Responsibilities and Recommendations for Changes

At the outset, I want again to emphasize that over my career I have been privileged to work with some extraordinary trustees. They have been deeply committed to and genuinely informed about higher education and the institutions on whose boards they sit. I have especially admired board chairs who have served generously as treasured advisors to their president, who have become assets to their institutions because of their focus on strategy and policy, and who have earned the respect of the faculty. I also have special and deep respect for several board chairs I know who have handled unanticipated crises at their institutions with both wisdom and grace.

Nevertheless, I have been struck by the number of highly publicized cases in the past several years of boards that have quite dramatically failed to fulfill their fiduciary responsibilities and in so doing have caused significant harm to their campus. In these instances, they have ignored their responsibilities as a governing board. Often they have not provided appropriate guidance to and oversight of the president. They have failed to ask basic questions and to monitor institutional performance in such key areas as finance and enrollment. These boards have tended without hesitation to accept presidential narratives and presidential decisions.

Although higher education historically is, I am sure, replete with examples of boards that have been similarly ineffective, today the mainstream media, along with social media, are casting a newly bright and often unrelenting spotlight on such problems.

In this chapter, I will offer some cautionary tales about board actions and inaction. I will describe ways that boards have both effectively and not effectively handled concerns about the president and discuss how to best handle the worst fear of most boards: that they will need to ask for a president's resignation or even to fire the president. I will also make some recommendations for boards about how they can fulfill their governance role more effectively.

Examples of Boards Failing to Provide Oversight

The boards of both Birmingham Southern College and the State University of Pennsylvania (Penn State) failed to provide appropriate oversight of the president and other senior members of the administration, who for their parts had made decisions detrimental to their institutions.

Birmingham Southern College

After being confronted in August 2010 with significant institutional financial problems, the board of Birmingham Southern College acknowledged that it had failed to provide appropriate oversight for the president and the senior members of the administration. In a statement released to the public, board chair Dowd Ritter attributed the board's ineffectiveness to the fact the board was too large, with sixty-one members. He also observed that twelve trustee committees was too many. Although Ritter did not put it this way, it appeared that because various aspects of oversight resided in so many different committees, no one was assuming responsibility for the institution as a whole.

The college found itself with a $13 million deficit on a total operating budget of $50 million. Several factors over a number of years contributed to the deficit:

- The college had borrowed heavily to finance upgrades to the physical plant.

- Although the college had, as it had hoped it would, increased enrollment by several hundred students to a high of 1,500, it also for years had spent far more on financial aid than budgeted, thereby leading to a reduction in net tuition revenue.

- In order to cover the shortfall created by discounting tuition more than budgeted, the finance department—without reporting it to the trustees or having the financial statements audited—had borrowed to make up the difference.

- During the recession, Birmingham Southern had not cut expenses but rather had increased salaries and other levels of spending, also based on the plan to increase enrollments.

- The college's finance department overstated revenues and understated expenses.

- Moody's downgraded the college's bond rating.

- Although no one was accused of fraud, Birmingham Southern violated federal guidelines by overawarding financial aid.

Even though the board announced that finance and financial aid administrators were responsible for this situation, rather than President G. David Pollick, the president resigned, saying that he did not want to be a distraction. Nevertheless, the case raises important governance questions about the president's role in overseeing senior administrators and also about the board's role in ensuring that the institution follow best practices, like annual independent audits conducted by a reputable firm external to the campus that reports directly to the board.

The fallout from these financial problems for the college was substantial. In order to reduce expenses by $10 million (one-fifth of the operating budget), the college laid off fifty-one staff members, did not fill fourteen staff vacancies, phased out five academic programs, and eliminated twenty-nine faculty positions. Birmingham Southern also reduced faculty and staff salaries by on average 10 percent. The college put its contribution to retirement plans on hold. The college offered early retirement packages for eligible faculty and staff.

Several high-ranking employees in the finance and financial aid department resigned in June. As Ritter also explained in his letter, the board took a number of steps to provide oversight. It created the position of controller and brought in financial advisors to design better practices and policies. A group of trustees, the interim president, and trustee leaders met weekly to address problems and improve communications. A trustee committee was constituted to study governance matters, including the board's size and how it structured itself and its committees.

Without the overawarding of financial aid, enrollment dropped. The college's website listed 1,305 enrolled students in fall 2012.

Pennsylvania State University

Penn State's handling of the Jerry Sandusky case is another example of the damage that can occur when a board fails to fulfill its fiduciary responsibility to provide oversight of a president who, according to the 2012 Louis Freeh report, for his part also failed to fulfill his own responsibilities for the university he led. The complacency of the Penn State board was especially serious because, if the Freeh report was accurate, such complacency allowed the president and the members of his senior administration to act in ways that jeopardized children coming on campus.

The Freeh report starkly reported these accumulating failures:

Four of the most powerful people at The Pennsylvania State University—President Graham B. Spanier, Senior Vice President-Finance and Business Gary C. Schultz, Athletic Director Timothy M. Curley and Head Football Coach Joseph V. Paterno—failed to protect against a child sexual predator harming children for over a decade. These men concealed Sandusky's activities from the Board of Trustees, the University community and authorities. They exhibited a striking lack of empathy for Sandusky's victims by failing to inquire as to their safety and well-being, especially by not attempting to determine the identity of the child who Sandusky assaulted in the Lasch Building in 2001. Further, they exposed this child to additional harm by alerting Sandusky, who was the only one who knew the child's identity, of what McQueary saw in the shower on the night of February 9, 2001.

These individuals, unchecked by the Board of Trustees that did not perform its oversight duties, empowered Sandusky to attract potential victims to the campus and football events by allowing him to have continued, unrestricted and unsupervised access to the University's facilities and affiliation with the University's prominent football program. Indeed, that continued access provided Sandusky with the very currency that enabled him to attract his victims. Some coaches, administrators and football program staff members ignored the red flags of Sandusky's behaviors and no one warned the public about him (pp. 1–15).

Graham Spanier resigned as president in November 2011 and became a member of the faculty on paid administrative leave (with an annual salary of $600,000 and a roughly $2.5 million package that included severance, deferred compensation, and retirement pay). In the summer of 2013, Spanier initiated a libel and defamation suit against Freeh. Shortly after that, a Harrisburg district trust judge ruled that evidence provided by state prosecutors was enough to warrant putting Spanier, Penn State's former athletic director, and its former vice president for finance and business on trial on charges of perjury, endangering the welfare of children, obstructing justice, conspiracy, and failure to report suspected child abuse.

By the summer of 2013, the scandal had cost the university nearly $48 million, mostly in legal and consulting fees. The NCAA imposed an array of sanctions, including a $60 million fine, vacating more than one hundred football victories, dropping Paterno from a list of top coaches, limiting football scholarships, and banning Penn State football for four years from participating in postseason bowl games.

The Penn State board of trustees spent the year following the Freeh report implementing almost all of Freeh's 119 recommendations for overhauling governing and reforming how the board and the university functioned. For example, the university hired its first academic integrity officer and its first director of ethics and compliance. It trained 16,000 people (some in person and others online) about their responsibility to report suspected child abuse. The university trained campus security staff and others about their duties under the federal campus safety law.

Keith E. Masser, the chair of the Penn State board, told the *Washington Post* in July 2012 that the process of implementing the Freeh recommendations has made the university "more efficient, more transparent and more accountable." He added that the goal was to "ensure that our institution never again has to ask whether it did the right thing or whether more could have been done."

UVa Board Ignores Best Practices of Governance

A highly publicized conflict over a board's approach to governance in recent years occurred at the University of Virginia (UVa) when in June 2012 the board of visitors asked UVa's relatively new president Teresa Sullivan to resign.

Sixteen days later, in response to a great deal of pressure from UVa faculty, students, alumni, and a former rector (aka board chair) in a well-orchestrated campaign and shortly after Governor Bob McDonnell told the board it needed to resolve the situation or he would remove all the trustees, the board voted unanimously to reinstate Sullivan. Vice Rector Kington resigned from the board. McDonnell then reappointed Rector (aka board chair) Helen E. Dragas to a second four-year term on the board, although she is no longer rector.

Only Dragas, Kington, and perhaps the four other members of the executive Committee of the Board of Visitors know for sure what prompted the decision to ask the highly regarded and experienced Sullivan for her resignation as she was completing her second year of a five-year contract as the University of Virginia's president. But interviews with some of the players suggest that Dragas and other key board members were reportedly influenced by Christensen and Eyring's advocacy of disruptive innovation and had become persuaded that President Sullivan was not moving quickly enough to bring about changes that these board members had concluded were essential.

College and university presidents clearly serve at the pleasure of their boards, and in fact the most important responsibility of boards is to hire and in unfortunate cases to fire presidents. But what seemed to elude the UVa board was that when boards decide to terminate a presidential appointment, they have the responsibility to do so in a way that is informed, adheres to institutional and legal processes, and is ethical. Boards also have the responsibility to act in ways that they are convinced will not harm the institution.

The public record is absolutely clear that the UVa board did not fulfill its fiduciary responsibilities when it agreed to Sullivan's resignation. Neither the full sixteen-person board nor even its six-person executive committee met to deliberate fully about what is inevitably a momentous decision in the life of a college or university: a forced presidential resignation. Rather, Dragas reportedly contacted most board members individually and thus elicited their support one by one. Three board members have reported that they had not even been consulted about the decision in advance, but rather informed of it only after Dragas had gained commitments from other board members for the necessary votes. The three did, however, indicate that they acquiesced in the decision.

In addition, after President Sullivan tendered her resignation, only three of the six executive committee members attended the meeting to accept her resignation. The board also ignored best practices by voting to fire President Sullivan without first formally evaluating her and again without sharing with her any board concerns.

The board's action was a public relations disaster for the university. In the days following Sullivan's resignation, two faculty groups took votes opposing the board's actions. Some faculty members contemplated a faculty "walkout." Alumni threatened to discontinue giving to the university unless Sullivan was reinstated. Hunter R. Rawlings III, president of the Association of American Universities and former president of Cornell University, was unequivocal in his condemnation of the board's action, telling the *Washington Post* on June 13, 2012: "This is the most egregious case I have ever seen of mismanagement by a governing board. It's secretive, it's misguided and based on the public statements, there is no clear rationale."

Illinois Board Ignores Conflicts of Interest

In the summer of 2009, most of the members of the University of Illinois board of trustees resigned at the request of the Illinois Admissions Review Commission because of their inappropriately influencing the admissions processes at the university. Specifically, a *Chicago Tribune* investigation found evidence that from 2005 to

2009, the administration gave preferential treatment for admissions to students connected with members of the board, elected officials, and major donors. The investigation also found evidence in public records that trustees had attempted to influence admissions nearly one hundred times in three years and that despite the objections of the admissions staff, some of those applicants (including friends and relatives of trustees) were admitted.

Governor Pat Quinn then appointed a panel to investigate what became known as "the clout scandal." The panel, which issued its report in August, was critical of White, Herman, and the trustees. The panel also called for the resignation of all members of the board of trustees, an overhaul of the admissions process, and new ethics policies for the board.

Before the report was issued, according to a July 13, 2009 piece in the *Chronicle of Higher Education*, "Backlash Over U. of Illinois 'Clout' Scandal Spreads to Trustees and News Media," "two former presidents of the University of Illinois system and two former chancellors of the flagship campus said the Board of Trustees had laid the groundwork for flaws in the admissions process by undermining administrators and meddling in operational decisions, including admissions." These former administrators charged that some trustees "pursued personal interests and saw themselves accountable only to the governor." They further claimed: "The power and authority of the university's administration were eroded, and some trustees delved into operational decisions across a broad spectrum including admissions." Some observers believe that the trustees thought that gaining admission for students they favored was simply a perquisite of being a trustee.

The *Chicago Tribune*, in a September 24, 2009 article, "University of Illinois President B. Joseph White Resigns," described the outcome of the panel's investigation this way:

[The panel] criticized White for failing to oversee his subordinates and for acting unethically in forwarding admissions requests. For example, in 2005, White was found to have forwarded a request initiated by Gov. Rod Blagojevich to admit a relative of convicted influence peddler Antoin "Tony" Rezko. The student, who was to be rejected, was instead admitted.

White responded that he did not know Rezko and had never forced anyone to admit a student. White then initiated an overhaul of the admissions system and apologized for the earlier abuses. The university's faculty and student senates, nevertheless, passed resolutions calling for both White and Urbana-Champaign chancellor Richard Herman to be removed from office. White soon after resigned, earning praise for forgoing a $475,000 retention bonus. He became a member of the faculty in business, earning about $300,000 per year.

The panel concluded that Herman played an even more active role. On October 20, 2009, the *Chicago Tribune*, in a piece entitled "Richard Herman, U of Illinois Chancellor, Resigns After Scandal," reported Herman's activities this way:

> In e-mails released by the university and in news reports since May, it became clear that Herman played a key role in what the university called its Category I list—students with political connections whose applications for places at the flagship Urbana-Champaign campus were closely tracked. Some of those applicants were admitted over more qualified ones.
>
> In some e-mails, Herman pushed for the admission of underqualified applicants to the university's law school and agreed to provide scholarship money in exchange … Herman has said he didn't believe he had the power to end a system of influence that predated him and was ingrained in the state's political culture.
>
> Herman resigned in October and joined the math department as a faculty member.

Seven of the trustees resigned and the governor made new appointments. In January 2013, Governor Quinn appointed former US attorney Patrick Fitzgerald to the university's board of trustees. Fitzgerald is well known nationally for fighting corruption and had successfully prosecuted former governor Blagojevich.

Other Boards That Have Not Avoided Conflicts of Interest

I know of other boards that have not understood the importance of their adhering to a conflict-of-interest policy, to the detriment of the institution. A few examples will make the point:

• A private university found itself in financial difficulty after having relied for decades almost exclusively on the investment advice of a financial consultant who was also a trustee. The consultant had favorite investments and did not seek the sort of diversification that characterizes most college and university portfolios. The other trustees on the board provided no oversight of the investments because they feared that doing so would insult their fellow trustee. The other trustees also were hopeful that this trustee would make a major gift to the institution in the future. The board finally became involved when it learned that the university had a several-million-dollar structural deficit. That deficit led to approximately forty faculty and staff members being laid off as well as other significant cuts.

• A private university board had deliberately established no formal bidding process, believing that granting contracts to trustees enabled the institution to attract to the board people who might not otherwise be interested. The assumption was that the trustees would be fair in establishing their prices and also would be apt to make gifts to the college. A new president discovered that neither of those assumptions proved to be true. He persuaded the board that it needed a policy establishing a formal bidding process for contracts.

- The trustee of another university decided that he did not need to pay the tuition for his son and daughter. He believed that his service as a trustee should be enough. The president was wise enough to ask his board chair to intervene. The trustee eventually paid. This same trustee became enraged when his son was arrested for an on-campus altercation with another student. After he bailed his son out of jail, he called the president at home at 6 a.m. to demand that the president immediately fire the dean of students, who he believed should have intervened with the police and prevented the arrest. The president refused. The trustee turned his anger on the president but remained on the board for the remaining several years of his term, often opposing the president.

Boards Ignore Faculty Discontent with the President

Several years ago, an experienced board chair, faced with the faculty's vote of no confidence in a president whom he and other trustees admired, immediately convened the board. The board accepted the president's explanation that the faculty was resistant to all changes and objected to his desire to raise standards. As was the case with a number of the examples cited in chapter 5, the board announced publicly that it had full confidence in the president. Moreover, on the chair's recommendation, this board, ahead of schedule, extended the president's contract for an additional five years.

Some of the trustees saw the faculty's vote as an act of insubordination and wanted to ask the protesting faculty to resign, despite the fact that these faculty members were tenured. In their anger, these trustees overlooked that fact that prior to the arrival of the current president, they had had great respect for the faculty. These trustees also overlooked the realities that most members of the faculty would be at the institution longer than the president, that most of them were deeply committed to their work and their students, and that the faculty is essential to the institution's fulfilling its educational mission.

The campus became deeply divided. Candidates for both administrative and faculty positions withdrew from consideration. Some alumni decided to withhold gifts. The public protests took a toll on admissions and retention. Friendships between faculty members and trustees, some of whom had been the students of those faculty members, became frayed.

The situation was resolved when the longtime chair retired and the new chair decided quietly to look into some of the allegations made by faculty members. He told the president that he was doing so. In the process, he began to believe that there had indeed been some fire that had inspired all the smoke. For example, he learned that the president had exaggerated the amount of money he had raised. After the chair discussed his concerns privately with the president and then with the executive committee, the president chose to retire for personal reasons.

The faculty members of a regional comprehensive university similarly found themselves with a president in whom they had no trust. They believed that he had fired several of their colleagues for being critical of him. Some of those colleagues had sued. Two had gone to the American Association of University Professors (AAUP), which sent a team to campus and ultimately put the institution on the AAUP censure list.

Worried that negative publicity would harm the institution, the faculty decided not to take a vote of no confidence. Instead, senior faculty members began to talk privately with trustees who were graduates of the institution and whom the faculty members therefore knew personally. The board at first ignored both the faculty's concerns and the AAUP censure. The president had convinced the board that the faculty was made up of anarchists and that the AAUP was a subversive organization that had no standing in the higher education community.

Many faculty members became demoralized by what seemed to them to be the trustees' failure to appreciate their concerns and that of the AAUP.

Several years later, a new board chair and the president went to a workshop on governance, which advised that it was a best practice for colleges to retain a consultant to conduct a 360-degree evaluation of their president. The new chair hoped that such an evaluation would help the president play to what he and other trustees thought were the president's strengths and to help him and board determine ways to compensate for his weaknesses, perhaps through a staff reorganization.

The consultant quickly discovered that the problems were far more significant than the board had recognized. He reported to the trustee committee overseeing the evaluation that the president had directed the vice presidents to withhold or to shade information about the budget and enrollment that went to the board, telling the vice presidents that he would fire them if they did not do his bidding. The board chair, armed with the consultant's report, met with the president, who initially denied the accusations. The chair then shared the report with the executive committee, which instructed the university's attorney to advise the president that the board intended to fire him for cause. At that point, the president resigned, citing health issues.

The board, now alarmed by its lack of knowledge of what had been taking place on the campus, brought in a retired president as interim for a year and charged her with creating policies and practices that were collaborative and transparent. The trustees were startled to learn from their interim president that being censured by the AAUP could negatively affect the college's bond rating. They were also startled to learn that the AAUP censure had already affected faculty and staff hiring and retention. The interim president worked with the board to devise ways that it would provide better oversight. This board began its search for a new president believing that it now understood its role.

Lessons Learned

Most of the boards described in this chapter recognized only after facing a crisis that they needed to reevaluate their role. Each brought in an expert on governance to facilitate a workshop, usually of a day or two in length, to help the trustees understand what it meant to have fiduciary responsibility. Each board focused on its conflict-of-interest policy. Like the Penn State board, each committed to requiring greater transparency and greater accountability for the campus and for themselves. Each identified the information that they wanted to receive routinely from the administration, in what form, and how often.

Recommendations for Boards

Recommendation 1: Trustees Must Be Actively Engaged

Trustees today need to do more than just "come for lunch" and bask in the prestige that being a board member often brings them. That level of complacency may have worked in the past for institutions with effective presidents and particularly in a time of ample resources. Today, however, as a number of the cautionary tales in this book illustrate, colleges and universities suffer, often mightily, when their trustees fail to take seriously their fiduciary responsibility for the institution's health and integrity.

Recommendation 2: Trustees Must Be Informed in Order to Serve as the President's Strategic Partners

To provide the president with beneficial advice, trustees need to understand the institution's challenges and opportunities and the possible strategies to address both. They need to be informed about trends in higher education.

Recommendation 3: Trustees Need to Understand and Appreciate the Good Work That Faculty Do

In my experience, it serves trustees well if they understand what it requires for faculty members to teach well; provide valuable institutional service (including advising students on an array of matters, from the courses they take to career and graduate choices); engage in scholarly, research, and creative activities; and even write letters of recommendation for students. Trustees will better appreciate the work of the faculty if they understand how many hours it takes to prepare a class, grade papers and exams, and meet individually with students. Trustees may be more sympathetic to concerns that faculty members express about institutional decisions when they, as trustees, understand the service expectations of faculty. They may also better understand that most faculty do not have their summers off but rather spend that time engaged in the scholarship, research, or creative pursuits that their role as professor demands.

Trustees also, I believe, need to understand the academic culture (peculiar as it may seem to some of them, because colleges and universities are very different from the organizations from which most of them come) so that they can work effectively not only with the president but also with the faculty and sometimes the students and the alumni to bring about needed change.

In discussions about governance, I often hear trustees question the tenure system. These trustees worry that the guarantee of lifelong employment enables faculty members to avoid being accountable for either their performance or for their actions. My experience tells me otherwise. Perhaps because their students judge faculty members almost daily, most faculty members care deeply about and work at being good teachers. Perhaps because faculty who teach at colleges and universities with expectations for scholarship and research are judged both by their immediate peers and their peers at other institutions, most faculty members care deeply about producing worthy work.

Recommendation 4: Boards Need to Establish a Regular Process of Presidential Evaluation

Hiring and evaluating presidents is, in my judgment, a board's most critical responsibility. In the best of all worlds, the board chair makes it clear to a new president, at the time of appointment, the process that the board intends to use to evaluate that president's performance. Ideally, the campus also understands the nature of the process, although only the board should be privy to the results of such evaluations. I recommend this approach so that, for example, when the board periodically conducts a 360-degree evaluation that involves members of the campus community, the campus will understand that this is a standard practice and not a sign of a problem with presidential performance.

In specific terms, I recommend that the board leadership and the president every summer agree on the president's top five or six goals, prepared in writing, for the coming year, which the president also shares with the full board. I further recommend that in the ensuing summer, the president share, also in writing, his or her evaluation of progress toward those goals as well as the slate of goals for the coming year.

Finally, I think that it makes sense every four or five years for the board to retain a consultant external to the institution to conduct a 360-degree evaluation with the purpose of providing the president with constructive advice. I hasten to add that both the president and the board, however, need to understand that if the board learns of serious performance problems, it may decide to act on them.

The Complexity of Terminating a President

Even if terminating a president is warranted, doing so is often unsettling for a college or university. For example, hiring a new president typically takes six months to a year or more, often putting the campus into a holding pattern by putting strategic planning processes, campaigns, and even the hiring of senior administrators on hold. In such situations, some institutions have turned to either a respected member of the administration or sometimes the board or to a retired president from a comparable kind of institution to serve in the interim position. In the best of circumstances, the interim president is able very quickly to restore trust, solve some key (often personnel) problems, and create a healthier environment for the next president.

Nevertheless, terminating a president may lead potential donors, fearing institutional instability, to withhold gifts. Other potential donors may simply want to wait to make a gift to be sure that they will support the views and values of next president. Some foundations, such as the Arthur Vining Davis Foundations, will not fund an institution until its president has completed at least his or her first year.

Recommendations for Boards That Are Confronted with Concerns About Presidential Performance

Recommendation 1: The Entire Board Needs to Be Involved in Decisions to Remove a President

One of the major lessons from the UVa debacle was that for an action of the magnitude of even considering terminating a president, the full board should base its decision on a full and fair evaluation of the president in terms of agreed-upon objectives and board expectations. The board also should meet in person, and the trustees together should debate the costs and benefits of the various options. In some circumstances, it would make sense for the executive committee first to engage in such deliberations prior to making a recommendation to the full board, which nevertheless should then also engage in its own considered deliberations before taking action.

The important piece here is that the board members deliber-ate as a group, each benefiting from the knowledge, insights, and judgments of others. I have seen many instances in which individual board members come to a meeting intending to vote in a particular way about a matter before them, only to be persuaded by the arguments of their colleagues to vote in a very different way.

In brief, a decision about whether or not to continue a president's service is such a critical one that not only should no small group of trustees be permitted to dictate board action, but in fact every single trustee should be actively involved in the deliberations.

Recommendation 2: All Discussions of Presidential Performance Must Be Informed

Prior to board deliberations about presidential performance, it is incumbent for those trustees charged with presidential evaluation to gather as much pertinent information as possible and to inform the president that they are doing so. For example:

- If the issue at hand is a disagreement over policy, I recommend that the president be allowed to explain first to the board leadership and then to the full board the basis for his or her stance. If at the conclusion of these discussions, the president and the board remain at odds, and the board, the president, or both choose to terminate the relationship, the decision will have been reached with full knowledge and, I would hope, with understanding and mutual respect.

- If the board has a concern about possible illegal activities, I recommend that appropriate trustees, like those in two of the examples later in the chapter—after discussing their concerns with the president and giving the president an opportunity to respond—emulate the trustees described in these examples by hiring an attorney versed in higher education to conduct, with the president's knowledge, a confidential and discreet investigation.

- If there are claims of inappropriate presidential behavior, I again recommend that appropriate trustees discuss these claims with the president, again giving him or her an opportunity to respond and then if necessary hiring someone qualified to investigate.

• Even in cases when a president admits culpability and chooses to resign, if the charges are of either illegal or immoral behavior, I suggest that the board nevertheless hire an investigator so that the board can be sure that it understands the full extent and implications of the inappropriate presidential behavior.

Recommendation 3: Boards Should Investigate All Signed Complaints About the President

A board that disregards or dismisses the concerns coming from the campus about the president (or any other matter) without investigating serves neither the institution nor its president. However, I think that the board should let it be known that it disregards all anonymous complaints.

How the board conducts its investigation, as the examples in this section illustrate, can be critical.

As a first step, the board chair should immediately inform the president of any concerns that come to the board's attention, even as the trustees preserve confidentiality related to the complainant. If the president is the subject of the complaint, the board needs to ask the president for his or her version of events. If the president is not the subject of the complaint and depending on the circumstances, the board might wish to delegate the investigation to the president. I also urge presidents to make their board aware of any concerns about the president's performance that the faculty has brought to the president's attention.

Again, in cases when claims are made about illegal, immoral, or potentially destructive actions, the board should retain someone from outside the institution to investigate. In cases where there are possibilities of illegality, I recommend that the board turn to a lawyer versed in higher education law.

Two stories will illustrate a successful process.

A Faculty Member Claims Discrimination

A faculty member at a well-known university, through her attorney, informed the board and the president that she was considering bringing suit, accusing the president of discriminating against women on campus. The board chair immediately consulted with the university attorney and then the two of them met with the president.

The president was able at this meeting with the board chair and the attorney to share with them statistics that demonstrated that he had been responsible for hiring and promoting a disproportionate percentage of women during his tenure. The president further noted that the faculty member in question had been promoted recently, with his approval and without any hesitation on his part. Her salary was comparable to her male peers. The board chair and the attorney then met with the executive committee. He and the committee were satisfied that the claims were unwarranted.

The president, however, decided to be proactive. He therefore encouraged the board to bring in a consultant of its choice to interview individually and in confidence the vice presidents, the administration program directors, the faculty department chairs, and the student government officers. The board chair and the president agreed that the consultant would not ask specifically about the charges about the campus climate for women but rather would seek input on the president's general effectiveness. The president wrote a memo to the campus, explaining that since he had been in office for four years, he and the board agreed it would be a good time to have someone from outside the institution evaluate how well the university was doing.

A recurring refrain from those with whom the consultant met was that the president had successfully and effectively diversified the faculty and the staff, hiring, promoting, and supporting not only women but also members of various ethnic minority groups and several openly gay people.

The university attorney shared both the information that the president had gathered and the consultant's report with the faculty member's attorney, who in turn shared them with his client. No legal action ensued.

A President Begins to Behave Erratically

A president who had been successful for more than a decade began to behave in ways that concerned the board. Indeed, the trustees observed that the president often became defensive and even angry when trustees questioned him or even asked for additional information, something that had not previously been the case. The board chair met privately with the president to talk about these concerns. The president vehemently challenged the validity of these perceptions. He did say that he wanted to stay for only a few more years and then would retire.

The executive committee of the board then decided—with the president's knowledge— that the university would retain a consultant to conduct a 360-degree evaluation, something it had not done previously. The ensuing report documented that the trustees' concerns were well founded and that the faculty leaders and senior administrators who had been interviewed as part of the evaluation were also worried that the president recently had exhibited anger in public. The consultant reported that most of those interviewed believed that it was time for the president to retire. The trustees agreed that the president's angry outbursts could be damaging to the institution over the longer term.

The board chair, acting at the behest of the entire board, and the president quickly came to an agreement that they would immediately announce the president's plans to retire in eight months, at the end of the academic year. The board quietly provided additional oversight of the president and immediately launched a national search for the next president. The board chair encouraged the president to seek counseling. All members of the board kept confidentiality about the consultant's report. The board held an all-campus reception that spring to thank the president for his service. The retired president returns for celebratory occasions to campus, where he is always greeted warmly.

A Board Fails to Inform the President About Complaints

In a different and instructive case, another board chose to investigate a complaint without first informing the president that it was doing so. Although the complaint in this case also turned out to be without merit, the board's response led the president to question whether she in fact had board support and to wonder whether she ought to look for a new position.

In this case, a dissatisfied male employee, who had taken a "buyout" and signed a release, nevertheless sent letters to a handful of trustees claiming that the president had discriminated against him because of his age and gender. The executive committee of the board met and decided that the board chair and another trustee should interview each of the vice presidents, the director of human resources, and the chair of the faculty senate to inquire whether the president was biased against men. The board did not inform the president either about the complaint or the plan to investigate. The chair and trustee asked those with whom they met to keep their conversation and the entire matter confidential.

The response in each case was that the president had been a strong advocate of equity of all kinds and that she had been extremely fair in her dealings with the faculty and staff. Members of her cabinet noted that four of the six vice presidents were men older than the president. Each indicated that he felt well supported.

Only after the investigation was concluded did the board chair formally inform the president about what had happened. The president shared with the chair her belief that it had undermined her authority for board members to talk with people who reported to her without her knowledge. Several of the vice presidents and the chair of the faculty senate independently shared with the president the fact that they had been uncomfortable with the conversation. Although the president and the board continued to work well together, the president continued to worry about the depth of the board's commitment to her.

Recommendation 4: Boards Should Seek PR Advice for Complex Situations

Boards need expert public relations advice if they intend to make a presidential change that is unexpected or potentially controversial, so that they can determine how best to announce and explain the change in leadership. The board chair should designate one person from the institution as spokesperson, whether that is the board chair, another trustee, or a member of the administration. All trustees, however, need to have a clear sense of what the messages will be even as they are cautioned not to discuss the situation, even in private conversations. The board chair should ask the press to work through the institution's communications person in scheduling interviews for the designated spokesperson, both because it is important to have the expertise of the communications person and also because knowing about an interview in advance gives the spokesperson an opportunity to prepare.

At UVa, a great many people (including the provost, the chief operating officer, the outgoing chair of the Darden Business School Foundation, and former administrators, as well as members of the faculty) spoke to the press. Because these commentators did not have actual information about the reasons for the board decision and so were able to share only their own opinions and sometimes speculation about what had happened, some of their remarks had the unintended consequence of adding to the uncertainty surrounding the situation. Although I do not believe it appropriate (much less possible) for colleges and universities to try to silence the faculty, staff, and students, the board and administration should literally speak with one voice.

Recommendation 5: If Possible, Boards and Departing Presidents Should Collaborate

A board that is confronted with a presidential transition (voluntary or involuntary) should collaborate if at all possible with the departing president both on the immediate press release and, just as important, on a long-term communications strategy. The board and the departing president will also need to bring the person in charge of the public relations into the loop. It may be that the board and the president, in the interest of transparency, can agree to disclose the nature of the disagreement between them. However, if the disagreement was about a personnel matter or if disclosing the area of disagreement might in itself prove harmful to the institution, I believe that the less said, the better.

Former UVa president Robert O'Neil described his transition out of the presidency more than two decades ago when, in his fourth year, he was told by some of the board members that they thought it was time for a change. Both he and the board handled the matter in an exemplary fashion. As the Charlottesville weekly, *The Hook*, reported on June 15, 2012, in "Bad Form? BOV Ignored Own President-Replacing Precedent," O'Neil was given the opportunity to meet individually with all board members and was the one to make the announcement in October 1989 that he would be leaving in December 1990 to take a new position. He also noted that he and his successor, John Casteen, "agreed on a date to pass the baton" and that their working together for nine months led to "a very orderly transition."

Recommendation 6: Boards Should Seek to Give Departing Presidents Dignity

Boards should also in every possible way give the departing president dignity as the relationship comes to an end. This is particularly true if, as Rector Dragas of UVa suggested was the case with President Sullivan, the rupture has to do with differences in approach to the nature and pace of change, or as Sullivan put it, "philosophical differences," rather than some sort of unethical, illegal, or even foolish behavior on the part of the president.

Recommendation 7: Personnel Matters Should Be Kept Confidential

All board members need to adhere to the notion that personnel matters are confidential.

Although I favor transparency when it is appropriate, Rector Dragas of UVa was right when, in the midst of the firestorm surrounding Terry Sullivan's resignation, Dragas stated that personnel matters are confidential. Virginia's sunshine laws, for example, permit a public body to "convene a closed executive session with a majority of the vote" for "discussions of employment, employment conditions, discipline and resignation of public employees." Virginia law does mandate that all votes be taken in open session, something that did not occur in the UVa case.

Ironically, in my judgment, Rector Dragas erred not by maintaining confidentiality but by violating it. In both her written and oral comments, she implied that President Sullivan was not advancing an agenda on key issues facing the university. For example, in Dragas's June 10, 2012 e-mail to the campus announcing the change, she wrote:

> The board feels strongly and overwhelmingly that we need bold and proactive leadership on tackling the difficult issues that we face. The pace of change in higher education and in health care has accelerated greatly in the last two years. The board believes this environment calls for a much faster pace of change in administrative structure, in governance, in financial resource development and in resource prioritization and allocation. We do not believe we can even maintain our current standard under a model of incremental, marginal change. The world is simply moving too fast.

In the interest of accuracy, I do want to note that President Sullivan prepared a lengthy memorandum to the board in May 2012 that provides considerable evidence that contrary to the rector's claims, Sullivan was in fact moving forward on a significant number of key issues.

Recommendation 8: Boards Should Clarify the Succession Plan

Before any public announcement is made about a presidential transition, the board should have developed and then should talk about the succession plan, particularly whether there is going to be an interim president and who that person will be, along with a description in broad strokes of the search process.

UVa's board created unnecessary anxiety by announcing that the provost and the chief operating officer would "run" the university until the board appointed an interim president.

Virginia governor Robert F. McDonnell, in a June 15, 2012 statement to the *Washington Post*—while announcing that he would not "meddle" in the affairs of the board—did push the board to make an immediate decision to name an interim president and move forward quickly with a search and a statement about the university's future, using the word "promptly" three times in one sentence:

> What I think, of course, is they need to promptly make a decision about an interim and promptly set up a very clear and transparent and open process about who will become the next president and they need to promptly engage the community, the faculty, and others . . . to explain what the future of Virginia holds.

Penn State, in contrast, handled the succession issue with great clarity. Simultaneously with the announcement of Spanier's resignation, the university announced that its provost, Rodney A. Erikson, would become interim president. Eight days later, the board removed the term "interim" from his title and named Erickson Penn State's seventeenth president. Then, less than two months later, Erickson announced that he would retire in the summer of 2014. The university has now embarked on a national search for its next president. The board apparently wanted the stability that Erickson

would bring as the university recovered from the scandal and insti-
tuted the necessary reforms to its policies and practices.

Recommendation 9: Board Leadership Should Communicate with the Campus

In conjunction with or immediately after making an announcement about a presidential transition, the board leadership should
meet with the leaders of key constituencies—the faculty, the staff,
the students, and the alumni—to inform them of the decision, to
explain the boundaries occasioned by confidentiality, and to out-
line the search process going forward.

Such an action would have avoided the sort of high drama that
occurred at Virginia about whether the Board of Visitors would
meet with faculty leaders, drama that was at the center of press
coverage.

Recommendation 10: Trustees Should Focus on the Institution

When commenting on decisions of institutional significance,
boards should keep their focus on the health and well-being of the
institution rather than on themselves.

I suspect that Rector Dragas did not earn sympathy for herself
or for the board when she said in her June 10, 2012 meeting with
the vice presidents and deans about the Sullivan presidency, "We
wanted it to work as well. That certainly would have been easier
on all of us."

Recommendation 11: Boards Need to Model the Core Values of the Institution

On June 15, 2012, the UVa student council wrote to the Board of
Visitors a statement eloquently making the point that the trustees
needed to embrace their institution's core values:

> The University of Virginia has a long and storied his-
> tory, one steeped with a strong sense of the values

upon which it was founded. Above all else, we belong to an institution of honor and honesty, of openness and respect. And it is under these values that we deem the current state of information on President Sullivan's departure wholly untenable. The University of Virginia community is entitled to more information. . . . The University of Virginia Student Council, as both representatives and members of the student body, respectfully requests a full explanation of the events and circumstances surrounding the departure of President Teresa Sullivan. Throughout the history of our institution, every student has been called upon to uphold the values of the University of Virginia. We the students are now calling upon the Board of Visitors to do the same.

Recommendation 12: Boards Should Try to Defuse Contentious Situations

Contentious situations tend to be idiosyncratic. Therefore, there is no one template for all such circumstances. In some instances, when confronted with concerns, after informing the president the board may simply choose to have informal conversations with those who express concerns. For example, in the case of a vote of no confidence, the board leadership might wish to meet with the leadership of the faculty simply to listen.

If there has been no immorality or illegality and if the president has been effective in a number of areas and still enjoys the confidence of the board, the board may direct the president to foster better communication and collaboration with the faculty.

Perhaps the best example I know of a board and president adeptly defusing a contentious situation centered on a president whom the board had explicitly hired to be a change agent. The faculty had agreed during the search that change was needed. On a number of levels, faculty found the president successful.

They were pleased that he was an effective fundraiser who had raised money for projects of great importance to the campus. The faculty credited him with being popular with both previously disenchanted alumni and with the students.

Nevertheless, a sizable number of faculty members had become alarmed in the president's second year that he was, despite what they knew to be the board's encouragement and support, moving too quickly. These faculty members complained that while he consulted widely, he did not appear to listen to his critics. These faculty members also believed that the president was ignoring provisions of the Faculty Code that he had argued were in conflict with the board's governing documents.

A delegation of faculty members went to the board chair with their concerns. She immediately met with the president to hear his version of the situation. Instead of becoming defensive, the president encouraged the chair to invite this small group of faculty to join her and the president for lunch, a gesture that reduced the level of tension for everyone involved.

After listening to the faculty delegation and then brainstorming with the group about what he might do to work more effectively with the faculty, the president at the next faculty meeting asked those in attendance to tell him how he could work with them more collaboratively. He then acted on their suggestions by making a concerted effort to meet with as many of them as possible. Although the campus was too large for him to consider one-on-one meetings, he began to invite faculty members to the president's house in small groups for meals and informal conversations. He also asked the faculty to select a representative group to work with him to clarify those aspects of the Faculty Code that the faculty claimed he was ignoring and to make the Faculty Code consistent with the board's governing documents. This committee, the president, and the provost then together worked hard for several months, reviewing faculty handbooks from peer institutions in order to come up with language and processes that worked for all parties. The faculty on the committee told their colleagues that they appreciated the time, energy, and care the president gave to this process.

The narrative on campus shifted. Many faculty members continued to worry that the president was moving too quickly, but they now felt consulted and had a better understanding of (and therefore a greater acceptance of) the decisions he was making. For his part, the president developed a new respect for the faculty—the work that they were doing and their commitment to their students. Perhaps even more important, he made it a point publicly and frequently to commend members of the campus community for what he considered exemplary performance.

This president was also candid with the board that focusing on matters of shared governance had taken what he considered an inordinate amount of time but that he had decided that it was time well spent. He also cautioned the board that this question about the pace of change would certainly arise again but that he intended to try to talk directly and routinely with the faculty about the reasons for his actions and to listen to their hesitations before making any decisions. In making this speech, he assured the board that he would try to work collaboratively with the faculty while continuing to make the decisions he thought necessary.

The next and final chapter will turn away from cautionary tales to exemplary tales and will make the case that even in difficult circumstances, institutions fortunate enough to have presidents who provide leadership and vision, supportive trustees, and faculty who collaborate with the administration can achieve positive transformation.

8

Exemplary Tales: Successful
Presidents

As I hope I've demonstrated, trustees, presidents, senior administrators, and faculty members all, to varying degrees depending on the circumstances, have critical roles to play in the governance of the institution. Even so, presidents more than anyone else determine the nature and pace of change on a campus. They also influence the tone and the nature of discourse on their campus and the level of collaboration and communication among the various constituents, including students, alumni, elected officials, and the local community as well.

In this chapter, I want to highlight four presidents who, although from diverse backgrounds, have made a profound difference at equally diverse institutions: Freeman A. Hrabowski III, University of Maryland, Baltimore County (UMBC); Robert McMahan, Kettering University; Laura Skandera Trombley, Pitzer College; and Vincent Maniaci, American International College (AIC).

Each of these presidents was selected with the hope that he or she would be a change agent. Each has benefited from collaborative and creative faculty colleagues and from supportive, dedicated trustees. Although each, I am sure, could recount contentious moments, overall these four presidents demonstrate higher education leadership at its most effective.

Kettering and AIC had been experiencing shrinking enrollment and budgetary deficits. Pitzer had long lived in the shadow of the other Claremont Colleges, with many feeling as though it was the poor cousin, regional rather than national in reach. All three institutions were tuition-driven. UMBC was founded in 1966. When Hrabowski became president in 1992, he outlined an ambitious vision for the institution, specifically that it would become a major research university, would attract and graduate African-American men in the STEM (science, technology, engineering, mathematics) disciplines, and would break down the walls between the campus and the community.

All four presidents have been successful for reasons that will become apparent in each of their stories, but perhaps most important, all of them were responsible for bringing to their institutions new resources that made it possible for them to begin to realize a new institutional vision. Within a year of McMahan's appointment, Kettering received a game-changing $15.5 commitment over three years from the Charles Stewart Mott Foundation and a grant from the federal Ignite Partnership that will bring Kettering and Flint approximately $750,000 in new, cutting-edge technology. Under Maniaci's leadership, AIC has significantly increased enrollment, both at the graduate and the undergraduate levels, by enrolling greater numbers of new students and significantly improving retention. Maniaci also raised money to make much-needed campus improvements. As noted in chapter 1, during the decade of Trombley's leadership, Pitzer has enjoyed a meteoric rise in its U.S. News & World Report ranking, has raised more than $100 million, and has built eight new buildings, all Leadership in Energy & Environmental Design (LEED) certified (four Gold and four Platinum). Hrabowski and his administration have secured the funds to complete nearly $700 million of capital projects.

Each of these presidents has earned the enthusiastic support of their boards, support that has been critical to their success and the success of their institutions. Although the issues facing public and private institutions have much in common, there are also important differences. Most notably, although private college presidents certainly work with elected and other public officials, presidents of private colleges turn to individuals, foundations, and corporations, rather than the state, for the bulk of funding for their institutions. The public presidents, on the other hand, rely a great deal on state support, financial and otherwise, as well as on private donations.

Each president has an impressive bio:

- Freeman Hrabowski graduated at age 19 from Hampton Institute with high honors in mathematics. He earned his MA and his doctorate in higher education administration/statistics from the University of Illinois at Urbana-Champaign. He is the coauthor of two books on enabling students of color "to beat the odds" and serves on an array of national boards. In 2012, President Obama appointed him the chair of the President's Advisory Commission on Educational Excellence for African Americans.

- Bob McMahan majored in art history and physics at Dartmouth, earned his PhD in physics from Duke, has been an entrepreneur and a policy advisor to the governor of North Carolina, and prior to coming to Kettering was dean of the School of Engineering at Western Carolina University and research professor of physics and astronomy at the University of North Carolina at Chapel Hill.

- Vince Maniaci earned a BA in sociology from Berkeley, a JD from the University of San Francisco, and an EdD from Penn. He came to his presidency after a successful career in fundraising at Occidental, Tulsa, and Bellarmine.

- Laura Skandera Trombley's degrees were all in English, her BA and MA from Pepperdine, and her PhD from the University of Southern California. Prior to coming to Pitzer, she was academic vice president and dean at Coe College and, before that, associate provost at SUNY-Potsdam. She is an internationally renowned Mark Twain scholar who has authored five books.

What follows is a more detailed description of what happened on each of their campuses.

The University of Maryland, Baltimore County

Freeman A. Hrabowski III became president of the University of Maryland, Baltimore County (UMBC) in 1992. Prior to that, as the institution's provost, he had worked with philanthropists Robert and Jane Meyerhoff to create the Meyerhoff Scholars Program, originally designed to encourage African-American men to study science and engineering. Over time, the program evolved and now supports students of color and women in the STEM disciplines. Other new programs at UMBC now extend into the arts and humanities. The institution, which enrolls 16,000 students at the graduate and undergraduate levels, describes itself as an "honors university."

The impact on this predominantly white public research university of the Meyerhoff and other programs, and the impact of Hrabowski's energy, passion, and commitment to innovation and entrepreneurialism, have been significant, as have been his unusually successful efforts to work in partnership with the faculty. Hrabowski has been especially committed to the notion that education transforms lives. He has also been committed to linking teaching and research, to challenging students to achieve at the highest level, and to creating a sense of community. Students insist that he knows their names and remembers the details of the sidewalk conversations he has had with them individually.

Since 1993, the Meyerhoff program has graduated more than 800 students and currently enrolls 300 undergraduate and graduate students. Meyerhoff graduates have earned 108 PhDs, 32 MD/PhDs, and 105 MDs from some of the nation's most prestigious institutions. More than 85 other alumni have earned graduate degrees in engineering.

Hrabowski also made good on his promise to break down the walls between the campus and the community. Today, UMBC's Research Park dedicates 71 acres on its 500-acre campus to more than eighty companies, many of them involved with information technology, biotechnology, and cybersecurity. UMBC students and faculty members work with these companies, gaining real-world experience as well as an understanding of entrepreneurialism.

In May 2013, President Hrabowski gave the William D. Carey Lecture at the Annual Forum on Science and Technology of the American Association for the Advancement of Science (AAAS), "Expanding America's Science and Technology Pipeline: Academic Innovation and Inclusive Excellence." In that lecture, he outlined the key principles and practices for the Meyerhoff Program, which clearly have informed his successful twenty-one-year presidency. He also said he drew "largely from best practices that [he] had observed and benefited from during [his] own undergraduate experience majoring in mathematics at Hampton Institute, and that mathematics professor Uri Treisman had identified in his research at the University of California at Berkeley on high-performing minority students in mathematics."

Specifically, Hrabowski and his colleagues understood that they would need to change the culture at UMBC. They began both by analyzing data about student performance in the STEM disciplines and by putting together focus groups of faculty members, staff members, and students to discuss "minority student underachievement in science and engineering." Hrabowski explained the emphasis on data this way:

> It is significant that while institutional culture reflects subjective values, culture change requires rigorous analysis: change begins when an institution looks carefully at itself, identifies its strengths and weaknesses, recognizes the challenges it faces, and understands that how it responds to those challenges can lead to desired outcomes.

He further argued that changing an institutional culture required creating a culture of assessment, which employs the same "scholarly rigor" expected of all researchers.

In this speech and elsewhere, Hrabowski identified the key components that he believes led to the program's success. These included actively recruiting the top students of color in math and science; using a rigorous selection process; requiring students to complete a six-week summer bridge program (that included, in addition to work in STEM disciplines, work in the humanities, problem solving along with group study, and an array of cultural and social events). He credited the faculty as being instrumental to the success of their students by being actively involved in recruiting, teaching, and mentoring them. Hrabowski also emphasized the importance of creating a culture that included "outstanding academic achievement, study groups, collegiality, and preparation for graduate school."

The Meyerhoff program engaged students in a variety of ways outside of the classroom. All students were involved in sustained and substantive research during the academic year and in the summer. They were encouraged to take advantage of available student support services, including tutoring, advising, and counseling. Students were linked to mentors from both the academic and the corporate world. Students were encouraged to engage in some form of community service. Their parents and other relatives were encouraged to be supportive of the students' efforts. UMBC administrators were actively involved in and fully supported the program.

The data from UMBC's ongoing and rigorous assessment efforts have been stunning. As Hrabowski noted in his AAAS speech:

> The Meyerhoff students were nearly twice as likely to persist and graduate in S&E [science and engineering] undergraduate majors; they achieved significantly higher S&E grade points averages; and the percentage of Meyerhoff students who graduated from or were attending S&E Ph.D. or M.D./Ph.D. programs was more than five times (5.3) greater than the percentage of "declined" students.

UMBC is now applying what it has learned from the Meyerhoff program to non-STEM areas and enjoying success in doing so. According to Hrabowski:

> The program also has been instrumental in creating an institutional culture embracing academic innovation and inclusive excellence. As we have seen, its success has led to other major campus initiatives, including a range of scholars programs for students with different interests, curricular changes in first-year STEM courses, and initiatives focused on both graduate student success and diversifying the faculty.

Freeman Hrabowski has won an impressive array of awards. He has raised money. He has earned the respect and support of Maryland's elected officials at all levels. He has built buildings. But most of all, he has inspired hundreds and hundreds of students who are now in their own lives committed to the transforming power of education.

Kettering University

Kettering University today has approximately 1,750 undergraduates and 330 graduate students and is rebounding from enrollment and financial problems. Although all Kettering students have a grounding in the liberal arts, Kettering students major in STEM disciplines and management. Kettering is also known for its commitment to experiential education expressed primarily in its distinctive, nationally recognized cooperative education program.

Founded in 1919 as the School of Automotive Trades, the institution in 1926 was acquired by General Motors as a training ground for future employees and eventually named "The General Motors Institute" or "GMI." General Motors heavily subsidized tuition. As part of a for-profit organization, GMI had no need to establish a tradition of philanthropy. The culture itself was corporate, not academic. GM spun off GMI, in 1982, giving the facilities to what became a new nonprofit private university, which was renamed "Kettering" in 1998.

Shortly after his arrival in August 2011, McMahan created an envisioning process that situated Kettering in the context of American higher education, asking the campus and the board to take into account the fact that higher education today is more collaborative and social than in the past, relies much more on peer-to-peer interaction, and is more virtual, with new technologies presenting both challenges and opportunities in terms of "delivering" education in ways previously unimagined. McMahan stressed that education must truly be student-centered and that it increasingly will be brought to students, rather than students coming to a brick-and-mortar school where they are passive recipients of knowledge presented to them. He argued that, to survive and flourish, traditional universities are going to have to evolve quickly and intentionally and that Kettering would need to be both "high tech" and "high touch."

McMahan's goal was action, but first he laid out his vision for Kettering's trustees, who gave him the encouragement he sought. He then created a process that invited input from the campus and that built on Kettering's rich history in the STEM disciplines and management and also on its co-op program. McMahan emphasized that the plan would need to document how Kettering would contribute to the economic vitality of Flint and the region, an area that had been significantly damaged by the 2008 downturn and problems in the automotive industry. By second semester, he had proposed an ambitious and integrated set of strategic priorities, which the board approved.

McMahan also was clear throughout the envisioning process that he advocated a process of ongoing and evolving planning rather than planning for a three-to-five-year time frame that produced a static plan.

In addition, even as McMahan was quite obviously listening and learning, he also had ideas that he wanted to test with the campus.

This approach did not work immediately, because many of his new colleagues assumed that if the president was advancing an idea, he had already made up his mind to implement it. Eventually, people understood that when McMahan said he wanted to brainstorm, he meant it. Faculty and staff who in the fall of his first year described to me on a visit to campus their skepticism about administrators soon became wonderfully forthcoming with ideas and opinions.

Based on what he learned during his intensive first three months, McMahan began making things happen. Determined to break down silos, create a team approach, and end bureaucratic practices that were legacies of the old GM culture, he reorganized the administration to make it more effective, responsive, and nimble. He made the head of information technology a vice president and charged her with reengineering processes to make them more effective and efficient. (Ending the requirement that purchasing requests had to be on handwritten forms with nine carbon copies was especially popular.) McMahan created a retention task force and by spring had appointed new vice presidents in finance and administration, enrollment management, and advancement. Kettering implemented a fixed-tuition guarantee for all undergraduates beginning in 2012–13. This summer Kettering upgraded dining facilities, expanded menus to include more custom-made items, and added a convenience store. Kettering also opened an Einstein Bros Bagels across the street from the campus and provided space in that same building for a Flint Police Service Center. The board of trustees, for its part, revised its by-laws and gave McMahan enthusiastic support.

As he was accomplishing all of this, McMahan drove his own staff crazy, because he kept overbooking his schedule. When some unhappy alumni shared concerns about a proposed initiative, he spent hours listening to them and then another hour winning them over. He spent countless hours wandering around the campus, talking to people. He had lunch often in the student center, joining students and quizzing them about their experience. He stopped by faculty offices, labs, and staff offices to ask about the work that people were doing and how he could help. He had lots of what I think of as "sidewalk conversations" as he walked unaccompanied across the campus. He met regularly with trustees, alumni, and potential donors.

A year later, McMahan still walks the campus, still has lunch with the students, still stops in faculty and staff offices to learn what people are doing and how he can help, and still meets with alumni as often as he can. He and the trustees work well together. He still is brimming with new ideas. He still regularly engages in brainstorming sessions with almost everyone he meets. Recently, he worked with the Genesee County Land Bank to purchase fifty tax-foreclosed parcels adjacent to the university with the option of buying seventy more at a cost of $100 a parcel. Kettering has demolished and rejuvenated the properties at its own cost as a way of contributing to Flint. The university was instrumental in creating a University Avenue Corridor Coalition to bring together area institutions, including two Flint hospitals, and area residents to work together to beautify this once rundown part of Flint. McMahan explains these initiatives this way: "We are not an island. Our success is tied to Flint's success. We have an obligation of service. One of the things we want to teach our students is community service."

And, yes, keeping on schedule continues to be a challenge for McMahan. But what is different now from a year ago is that Kettering is no longer just envisioning a brighter future but is making it happen.

American International College

American International College was founded in 1885 and chartered by the Commonwealth of Massachusetts with the purpose of educating international immigrants coming to America through New York. The AIC website puts it this way: "That's where our commitment to diversity, flexibility, and understanding began.

[These immigrants] came to America to pursue a dream and AIC was founded to ensure their success."

Today, AIC is a private master's university that describes its core as the liberal arts. The college comprises the School of Business, Arts & Sciences; the School of Health Sciences; and the School of Graduate & Adult Education. AIC offers master's degrees in business and nursing; doctorates in physical therapy, education, and educational psychology; and bachelor's degrees in all other areas. Located in the geographic center of Springfield, Massachusetts, AIC describes itself as "interracial, interfaith and international."

When Vince Maniaci joined AIC in 2005, he encountered an institution that for the previous decade had lost $22 million in operating expenses and at the time had a $5.3 million deficit. Enrollment was down. Retention was abysmal, with only 50 percent of first-year students returning for their second year. Expenses were still rising.

Maniaci was attracted to AIC because of its mission. Forty-five percent of its students are from ethnic minority groups. A majority are first-generation college students. Many are from low-income families. In other words, this is a population for which affordability is of great importance. Maniaci immediately decided that his focus and that of the college needed to be on attracting additional students and retaining those enrolled at much higher rates.

So that he could make immediate decisions with board support to address AIC's serious problems, Maniaci met weekly for his first year with the executive committee, which he calls "the A team." Frank Colaccino, AIC's board chair for the past six years, says that Maniaci has brought to the college enormous energy and creativity, an understanding of higher education, and a caring about people and that he was confident enough to welcome the expertise that the trustees brought in the financial and business arenas. For example, the board advised him about a defined benefit plan that, had it continued, would have increased rather than solved the deficit problem. Maniaci also reorganized his administration and made new senior appointments.

Today, the executive committee and Maniaci meet every other month. Although they are agreed that AIC has a long way to go, they have consistently enjoyed surpluses since Maniaci arrived and in 2013 celebrated the college's largest operating surplus (slightly more than $6 million). They also celebrated improved retention, increased enrollment, successful fundraising and some much-needed athletic facilities and fields, a renovated student center that includes a new bookstore, a convenience store, a coffee house, a campus living room, and a renovated library. AIC has begun to address deferred maintenance. Maniaci has put in place a plan to increase faculty and staff salaries.

AIC has made progress in other important ways. Freshman-to-sophomore retention has steadily improved, and this past year overall retention significantly surpassed the goal that had been set. When Maniaci arrived, undergraduate enrollment was 1,200. Today it's at 1,500, although Maniaci notes that three years ago this number was 1,750. Maniaci attributes this decline to the fact that the recession hit AIC's population of students especially hard. The number of graduate students over the same period has, however, increased from about 380 to more than 2,300. In 2012, the *Chronicle of Higher Education Almanac* ranked AIC the twelfth-fastest-growing institution among US private colleges offering master's degree programs.

Other accomplishments include the following: AIC has established new foreign and study abroad programs which both offer students opportunities to study and live in other cultures and are revenue producers for the college. In 2007, AIC rebuilt its entire technological infrastructure from scratch, situating the college among the most technologically advanced in the nation. Maniaci has also stressed the importance of public service for AIC students, who to date have logged more than 20,000 hours of public service. But perhaps most of all, Maniaci both created and then modeled a focus on AIC students. Every Friday morning on the campus green, he can be found tossing a football with any students who walk by. He knows almost every student by name. He improved the landscaping on campus, making it a place where students want to be. He changed campus dining so that faculty, students, and staff eat together. He added several new sports and hired full-time coaches, telling Springfield *Republican* reporter George Graham, "A full-time coach really helps you in terms of being able to recruit students and be there as a guiding force for students." He created a skating rink at the center of campus and joins the students in that activity.

Vince Maniaci is not content with where AIC is. He believes fervently in its mission, which he recognizes will require a significant infusion of new resources. However, he should take comfort from the fact that he may be the only college president in the country whose students created a Facebook page for him in which they declared that their president "rocks."

Pitzer College

When Laura Skandera Trombley became president of Pitzer in 2002, the college was ranked 70th among the national liberal arts colleges by *U.S. News & World Report*. While many national liberal arts colleges would covet this ranking, Pitzer inevitably compared itself to the other undergraduate colleges in the Claremont Colleges constellation—Pomona, Scripps, Claremont McKenna, and Harvey Mudd—which were national in draw whereas Pitzer was regional. The college had what Trombley characterizes as a "generous admissions policy" and dated buildings. Today, *U.S. News & World Report* ranks Pitzer 43rd, an extraordinary jump. The majority of the college's approximately 1,000 students now come from outside California; Pitzer is ranked among the twenty most selective colleges in the country and is ranked ninth among liberal arts colleges. The endowment in 2002 was $42 million; today it is at

$120 million. Retention has dramatically increased. Seventy-four percent of the class of 2013 studied abroad during their four years at Pitzer, half of them completing an independent project. Pitzer has become a national leader in terms of the number of Fulbright grants its students are awarded. Pitzer students, faculty, and staff contribute 100,000 hours in volunteer community service each year.

Why was Trombley so successful? First, when she arrived at Pitzer, she worked closely with a transition committee of students, faculty, staff, alumni, and trustees that helped her plan her first year. She believes that this committee, combined with her determination to listen to everyone she could, gave her a "window" into Pitzer's values, its culture, and its politics and also educated committee members about presidential responsibilities. Soon concluding that Pitzer was an excellent institution that hadn't shared the message about its excellence, the new president created an office of communication and public relations to craft and promote an integrated message. She also established the office of institutional research to help the college develop a culture of performance and accountability. The Pitzer trustees endorsed her hopes for the college.

Trombley also did three other things fairly quickly to create a sense of momentum: she created the college's first "excellence brochure," which she shared widely; she added two new faculty positions but tasked the faculty with determining their definition; and she moved into the president's house and then held a three-day open house, inviting everyone within a twenty-five-mile radius with some connection to Pitzer. She also did something that turned out to be critical. Because she wanted to communicate that the college was in fact moving forward, she turned to her board for immediate and important support. In response, six trustees raised about $330,000 to create an endowed scholarship fund in Trombley's name. The board has continued to be very philanthropic.

In her second year, Trombley focused on what she called tactical planning, in which the college defined and then began to address its most important needs for the coming five years. Pitzer also created a financial model that included anticipated net tuition revenue and fundraising totals. The college quickly met all of these goals and developed a new set of goals. The faculty then created a strategic academic plan that also was very goal-oriented.

As noted in chapter 1, by anticipating the economic recession and by cutting the operating budget by 5 percent in fall 2008 and making an unprecedented move to freeze endowment spending, Trombley was able to honor her commitment to "human capital." Unlike many institutions during the recession, Pitzer has neither laid off any faculty or staff members, has not cut financial aid, and continues to meet the full need of its students.

Pitzer now has the pride that Trombley wanted for it. The college's gardens were featured in *Los Angeles Times*. The college's students are considered among the happiest in the country, and they eat at one of the nation's top 10 healthiest dining halls. The college has become highly selective, admitting only 14.5 percent of applicants for the class of 2017. Thirty-one percent of last year's freshmen had a GPA of 4.0 or above. Trombley herself is proud that the board, faculty, and staff continue to be tolerant of change and willing going forward to continue to make careful, pragmatic, brave, and daring choices and to take measured risks.

Commonalities

Despite their differences and the different nature of their institutions, and in addition to raising money, each of these presidents did all of the following:

- Each actively and immediately engaged their boards, seeing them as strategic partners and benefiting from their moral and financial support.

- Each believed that their colleges were better than their reputations and better than their new colleagues and trustees recognized.

- Each was committed to listening but also was animated by ideas about how to address current problems and make their institutions better.

- Each inspired their faculty and staff colleagues and trustees to think about new programs, new ways of functioning, and brighter futures.

- Each led a process that developed a new institutional vision that was simultaneously forward-looking and grounded in what each president learned from colleagues, trustees, and alumni.

- Each respected the institution's history and core values.

- All were student-focused and spent a good deal of time talking with and listening to their students.

- All got to know members of their faculty and staff well.

- All did lots of walking around campus, having impromptu conversations with those they met along the way.

- Each was extremely transparent about the institution's fiscal situation.

Each of these stories should give us hope about the future of higher education even as they demonstrate the criticality of presidential leadership, the importance of committed trustees, and the essential role that faculty can and must play if their institutions are to thrive.

Resources

Bolman, Lee G., and Gallos, Joan V. *Reframing Academic Leadership*. San Francisco: Jossey-Bass, 2011.

Bowen, Jose Antonio. *Teaching Naked: How Moving Technology Out of Your College Classroom Will Improve Student Learning*. San Francisco: Jossey-Bass, 2012.

Brown, Alice W. *Cautionary Tales: Strategy Lessons from Struggling Colleges*. Sterling, VA: Stylus, 2012.

Chait, Richard P., Holland, Thomas P., and Taylor, Barbara E. *The Effective Board of Trustees*. New York: ACE Macmillan Series on Higher Education, 1991.

Christensen, Clayton M., and Eyring, Henry J. *The Innovative University: Changing the DNA of Higher Education from the Inside Out*. San Francisco: Jossey-Bass, 2011.

Morrill, Richard L. *Assessing Presidential Effectiveness: A Guide for College and University Boards*. Washington, DC: AGB Press, 2010.

Morrill, Richard L. *Strategic Leadership in Academic Affairs: Clarifying the Board's Responsibilities*. Washington, DC: AGB Press, 2002.

Trachtenberg, Stephen Joel, Kauvar, Gerald B., and Bogue, E. Grady. *Presidencies Derailed: Why University Leaders Fail and How to Prevent It*. Baltimore, MD: Johns Hopkins Press, 2013.

Trower, Cathy A. *The Practitioner's Guide to Governance as Leadership: Building High-Performing Nonprofit Boards*. San Francisco: Jossey-Bass, 2012.

References

American Association of University Professors (AAUP). *The Inclusion in Governance of Faculty Members Holding Contingent Appointments.* AAUP, January 2013. Available at http://www.aaup.org/report/governance-inclusion.

American Association of University Professors (AAUP). "Mission & Description." Accessed November 6, 2013. Available at http://www.aaup.org/about /mission-description.

American Association of University Professors. *1915 Declaration of Principles on Academic Freedom and Academic Tenure.* December 1915. Available at http://www.aaup.org/report/1915-declaration-principles-academic-freedom-and -academic-tenure.

American Association of University Professors and Association of American Colleges (AAC). *1940 Statement of Principles on Academic Freedom and Tenure.* Accessed November 6, 2013. Available at http://www.aaup.org/report /1940-statement-principles-academic-freedom-and-tenure.

American Association of University Professors, Association of American Colleges (AAC), and Association of Governing Boards of Universities and Colleges (AGB). *1966 Statement on Governance of Colleges and Universities.* Accessed November 6, 2013. Available at http://www.aaup.org/report/1966 -statement-government-colleges-and-universities.

American Association of University Professors (AAUP). *2010–11 Report on the Economic Status of the Profession.* Accessed December 16, 2013. Available at http://www.aaup.org/reports-publications/2010-11salarysurvey.

American Council on Education (ACE). "ACE Launches Presidential Innovation Lab." July 2, 2013. Available at http://www.acenet.edu/news-room/Pages /ACE-Launches-Presidential-Innovation-Lab-.aspx.

American Council on Education. "Leading Demographic Portrait of College Presidents Reveals Ongoing Challenges in Diversity, Aging." Washington, DC: ACE, March 12, 2012.

A Narrative Guide to the GustieLeaks Documents. Accessed November 6, 2013. Available at https://docs.google.com/file/d/0B8DTXaQod0ZqSE9BZkJtRVVf UnM/edit?pli=1.

Anderson, Nick. "Penn State Trustees: Governance Overhaul Nearly Done After Sandusky Sex Abuse Scandal." Washington Post, July 16, 2013.

"An Open Letter to Professor Michael Sandel from the Philosophy Department at San Jose University." April 29, 2013. Available at https://www.documentcloud .org/documents/695716-an-open-letter-to-professor-michael-sandel-from.html.

"A Radical Who Laid the Groundwork for the Tenure System: Scott Nearing, Professor." Wharton Alumni Magazine, Spring 2007. Available at http://www .wharton.upenn.edu/125anniversaryissue/nearing.html.

Armitage, David, et al. "Letter from 58 Professors to Smith Addressing edX." Harvard Crimson, May 23, 2013.

Arum, Richard, and Roska, Josipa. "Your So-Called Education." New York Times, May 14, 2011.

Associated Press. "Graham Spanier Sues Louis Freeh." ESPN College Football, July 15, 2013. Available at http://espn.go.com/college-football/story/_/id/9471461 /ex-penn-state-president-graham-spanier-sues-louis-freeh.

Balfour, Stephen P. "Assessing Writing in MOOCs: Automated Essay Scoring and Calibrated Peer Review™." RPA Journal. Available at http://www.rpajournal .com/assessing-writing-in-moocs-automated-essay-scoring-and-calibrated-peer -review/.

Barker, Tim. "SLU Faculty Votes No Confidence in Father Lawrence Biondi." St. Louis Post Dispatch, October 30, 2012.

Barren, Amanda. "University Faculty Vote Signals No Confidence in the President." Associated Press, May 1, 2013.

Bennett, William J., and Wilezol, David. "The Truth About College." Preface, *Is College Worth It?* Nashville, TN: Thomas Nelson, 2013.

Bérubé, Michael. "From the President: Among the Majority." *The Modern Language Association President's Blog.* Accessed November 6, 2013. Available at http://www.mla.org/blog?topic=146.

Birmingham-Southern College Office of Communications. "Birmingham-Southern College President David Pollick Steps Down, Board of Trustees Makes Other Major Announcements at Called Meeting." Press release, August 11, 2010. Available at http://www.bsc.edu/communications/news/2010/20100811 -pollick.cfm.

Boyers, Jason. "Why MOOCs Miss the Point With Online Learning." *Huffington Post,* July 4, 2013.

Bradbury, Alexandra. "Adjunct Faculty, Now in the Majority, Organize Citywide." *Labor Notes,* May 30, 2013.

Carlson, Scott. "Harvard's Debt Load Puts Strain on the University, Halts Projects." *Chronicle of Higher Education,* September 28, 2010.

Cohen, Jody S., St. Clair, Stacy, and Malone, Tara. "University of Illinois President B. Joseph White Resigns." *Chicago Tribune,* September 24, 2009.

"College Downsizes Departments, Phases Out Programs, Faculty, Staff." *Emory Wheel,* September 27, 2012.

David, Natalie Pullaro. *The 2012 NACUBO Tuition Discounting Study.* Washington, DC: National Association of College and University Business Officers, 2013.

DeSantis, Nick. "Morehouse College Won't Shut Adjuncts out of Obama's Speech After All." *Chronicle of Higher Education,* May 15, 2013.

De Vise, Daniel. "Are Va. College Trustees Groomed for Activism?" *Washington Post,* July 10, 2012.

De Vise, Daniel, and Kumar, Anita. "Teresa Sullivan Ouster: 33 Faculty Leaders Protest Her Dismissal from University of Virginia Presidency." *Washington Post*, June 13, 2012.

De Vise, Daniel, and Kumar, Anita. "U-Va. Board: President Teresa Sullivan's Removal Came after 'Extended' Talks Over School's Health." *Washington Post*, June 13, 2012.

Dickeson, Robert C. *Prioritizing Academic Programs and Services: Reallocating Resources to Achieve Strategic Balance*, revised and updated edition. San Francisco: Jossey-Bass, 2010.

Diel, Stan. "Financial Aid Error Costs Birmingham-Southern College Millions; Cuts Likely." *Birmingham News*, June 15, 2010.

Durkin, Connor. "Gallatin Professors Vote No Confidence in NYU President John Sexton." *NYU Local*, May 3, 2013.

Eckel, Peter D., Cook, Bryan J., and King, Jacqueline E. *The CAO Census: A National Profile of Chief Academic Officers*. Washington, DC: American Council on Education, 2009.

Editorial. "Missteps Mount for FAU's Saunders." *Sun-Sentinel* (Fort Lauderdale, FL), April 2, 2013.

"Emory Faculty Rejects Motion of No Confidence in President." Quick Takes, *Inside Higher Ed*, April 15, 2013.

"Endowment Value Declines 29.5% as Investment Return Is Negative 27.3%." *Harvard Magazine*, September 10, 2009. Available at http://harvardmagazine.com/2009/09/sharp-endowment-decline-reported.

Evans, Ivan. "When Adjunct Faculty Are the Tenure-Track's Untouchables," quoted in Christopher Newman's blog *Remaking the University*, May 19, 2013. Available at http://utotherescue.blogspot.com/2013/05/when-adjunct-faculty-are -tenure-tracks.html.

Fain, Paul. "Backlash Over U. of Illinois 'Clout' Scandal Spreads to Trustees and News Media." *Chronicle of Higher Education*, July 13, 2009.

Fain, Paul. "Birmingham-Southern's President Resigns While Trustees Explain College's Financial Meltdown." *Chronicle of Higher Education*, August 11, 2010.

Fain, Paul. "Phoenix Reloads." *Inside Higher Ed*, October 26, 2012.

Faulkner, William. *Requiem for a Nun*. New York: Vintage, 1950.

Florida Atlantic University, Office of the Provost. "Budget Conversation." Accessed November 6, 2013. Available at http://www.fau.edu/provost/budget _suggestions.php.

Freeh, Louis. *Report of the Special Investigative Counsel Regarding the Actions of The Pennsylvania State University Related to the Child Sexual Abuse Committed by Gerald A. Sandusky*. Freeh Sporkin & Sullivan, LLP, July 12, 2012. Available at http://progress.psu.edu/assets/content/REPORT_FINAL_071212.pdf.

Gaff, Jerry, "What If the Faculty Really Do Assume Responsibility for the Educational Program?" *Liberal Education*, vol. 93, no. 4, 2007.

Gerber, Larry. "Professionalization as the Basis for Academic Freedom and Faculty Governance." *AAUP Journal of Academic Freedom*, vol. 1, 2010.

Gillie, John. "PLU Fights Effort to Form Contingent Faculty Union." *News Tribune* (Tacoma, WA), April 30, 2013.

Global Credit Research. "One-Third of US Colleges Facing Falling or Stagnant Tuition Revenues." *Moody's Investors Service*, January 10, 2013. Available at http://www.moodys.com/research/Moodys-One-third-of-US-colleges-facing -falling-or-stagnant--PR-263437.

Global Credit Research. "Moody's: U.S. Higher Education Outlook Remains Mixed in 2012." *Moody's Investors Service*, January 23, 2012.

Harkness, Peter. "Public Universities Reach a Tipping Point." *Governing the States and Localities*, June 2012. Available at http://www.governing.com/topics /education/gov-public-universities-reach-tipping-point.html.

Hicks, George. "Letter to the Gustavus Community." Accessed on November 6, 2013. Available at https://docs.google.com/file/d/0B8DTXaQod0ZqWkhIQ0podn BNOE0/edit?pli=1.

Hrabowski, Freeman. "Expanding America's Science and Technology Pipeline: Academic Innovation and Inclusive Excellence." *The William D. Carey Lecture at the American Association for the Advancement of Science's Annual Forum on Science and Technology*, May 2, 2013. Available at http://umbc.edu/newsevents /careylectureaaas.pdf.

Ipsos Public Affairs. *How America Pays for College 2012: Sallie Mae's National Study of College Students and Parents, Conducted by Ipsos Public Affairs*. Accessed November 6, 2013. Available at https://www.salliemae.com/assets/Core/how -America-pays/HowAmericaPays2012.pdf.

Jaschik, Scott. "The Cost of Need Blind." *Inside Higher Ed*, February 25, 2013.

Jaschik, Scott. "Disappearing Languages at Albany." *Inside Higher Ed*, October 4, 2010.

Jaschik, Scott. "Rejected for Being In-State." *Inside Higher Ed*, August 13, 2012.

Jaschik, Scott. "Union Democracy for Some?" *Inside Higher Ed*, April 29, 2013.

June, Audrey Williams, and Newman, Jonah. "Adjunct Project Reveals Wide Range in Pay." *Chronicle of Higher Education*, January 4, 2013.

June, Audrey Williams. "Professors Seek to Reframe Salary Debate." *Chronicle of Higher Education*, April 8, 2012.

June, Audrey Williams. "Provost Who Sought Controversial Tenure-Review Policy at Saint Louis U. Will Step Down." *Chronicle of Higher Education*, December 17, 2012.

Kabbany, Jennifer. "Prof Who Said Newtown Massacre Didn't Happen Calls Boston Bombings 'Mass Casualty Drill'." *College Fix*, April 24, 2013.

Kaminer, Ariel. "Facing Criticism, N.Y.U. Will Cease Loans to Top Employees for Second Homes." *New York Times*, August 14, 2013.

Kaminer, Ariel. " 'No Confidence' Vote for Head of N.Y.U." *New York Times*, March 15, 2013.

Kapsidelis, Karin, "Head of Darden Board at U.Va. Resigns over Sullivan Email." *Richmond Times-Dispatch*, January 18, 2013.

Keeling, Richard, and Hersh, Richard H. *We're Losing Our Minds: Rethinking American Higher Education.* Palgrave Macmillan, 2011.

Kiley, Kevin. "Another Liberal Arts Critic." *Inside Higher Ed*, January 30, 2013.

Kiley, Kevin. "Debt by a Thousand Cuts." *Inside Higher Ed*, March 13, 2013.

Kiley, Kevin. "High Noon in Austin." *Inside Higher Ed*, March 7, 2013.

Kiley, Kevin. "Need Too Much." *Inside Higher Ed*, June 1, 2012.

Kiley, Kevin. "Short-Term Focus, Long-Term Problems: A Survey of Business Officers." *Inside Higher Ed*, July 27, 2012.

Kiley, Kevin. "Voting with No Confidence." *Inside Higher Ed*, May 23, 2013.

Kingkade, Tyler. "Scott Walker Calls for Shift in Higher Education Funding Tying Dollars to Completion Rates." *Huffington Post*, November 19, 2012.

Kolowich, Steve. "Into the Fray." *Inside Higher Ed*, July 17, 2012.

Kolowich, Steve. "A University's Offer of Credit for a MOOC Gets No Takers." *Chronicle of Higher Education*, July 8, 2013.

Kolowich, Steve. "Why Professors at San Jose State Won't Use a Harvard Professor's MOOC." *Chronicle of Higher Education*, May 2, 2013.

Kolowich, Steve. "Why Some Colleges Are Saying No to MOOC Deals, at Least for Now." *Chronicle of Higher Education*, April 29, 2013.

Kumar, Anita. "McDonnell Reappoints Dragas to U-Va. Board." *Washington Post*, June 29, 2012.

Lantigua, John. "Heated Questions, Muted Answers as FAU Defends Naming Stadium After Prison Company." *Palm Beach Post*, March 1, 2013.

Lederman, Doug. "CFO Survey Reveals Doubts About Financial Sustainability." *Inside Higher Ed*, July 12, 2013.

Lederman, Doug. "College Enrollments Fell This Fall." *Inside Higher Ed*, December 19, 2012.

Lederman, Doug. "We're Losing Our Minds." *Inside Higher Ed*, February 9, 2012.

Lende, Daniel. "Florida Governor: Anthropology Not Needed Here." October 11, 2011. Available at http://blogs.plos.org/neuroanthropology/2011/10/11/florida-governor-anthropology-not-needed-here/.

Levin, Tamar. "Universities Reshaping Education on the Web." *New York Times*, July 17, 2012.

Lipsitz, Ari. "Professors Decide Whether to Hold No Confidence Vote Against President Sexton." *NYU Local*, December 13, 2012. Available at http://nyulocal.com/on-campus/2012/12/13/professors-decide-whether-to-hold-no-confidence-vote-against-president-sexton/.

Luo, Michael. "N.R.A. Stymies Firearms Research, Scientists Say." *New York Times*, January 25, 2011.

Malone, Tara, St. Clair, Stacy, and Cohen, Jodi S. "University of Illinois: 4 More Trustees Offer to Quit." *Chicago Tribune*, August 19, 2009.

Marcus, Jon. "College Enrollment Shows Signs of Slowing." *The Hechinger Report*, May 31, 2012.

Margesson, Robert J. *A Rhetorical History of Academic Freedom from 1900 to 2006*. Ann Arbor, MI: ProQuest LLC (UMI Microform), 2008.

Martin, Andrew. "Building a Showcase Campus, Using an I.O.U." *New York Times*, December 13, 2012.

Mayo, Michael. "FAU Stadium Deal with Prison Company Geo Group Is Odd Way to Feather Nest: Owls' $6 Million Gift from Boca Raton Firm Is Ripe for Ridicule, Criticism." *Sun-Sentinel* (Fort Lauderdale, FL), June 22, 2012.

McDonnell, Robert. "Letter to UVa Board of Visitors." *Washington Post*, June 22, 2012.

McVicar, Brian. "Calvin College Cuts 22 Positions, Raises Health Care Costs to Pay Down $115 Million Debt." *MLive*, May 24, 2013.

Megerian, Chris, and Gordon, Larry. "Brown Wants to Tie Some Funding of Universities to New Proposals." *Los Angeles Times*, April 22, 2013.

Mercer, David. "Richard Herman, U of Illinois Chancellor, Resigns After Scandal." *Huffington Post*, October 20, 2009.

Metzger, W. P. *Academic Freedom in the Age of the University*. New York: Columbia University Press, 1955.

Meyer, Robinson. "What It's Like to Teach a MOOC (and What the Heck's a MOOC?)." *Atlantic*, July 18, 2012.

Miller, Ethan. "Struggling to Organize, Adjuncts Succeed at American University." *Labor Notes*, March 14, 2012.

Munk, Nina. "Rich Harvard, Poor Harvard." *Vanity Fair*, August 2009.

Murray, Robb. "President Shrugs Off Complaints." *Mankato Free Press* (Mankato, MN), May 29, 2009.

National Association of Independent Colleges and Universities (NAICU). "New Affordability Measures at Private, Nonprofit Colleges and Universities: Academic Year 2012–13." December 28, 2012.

National Association of Independent Colleges and Universities (NAICU). "New Affordability Measures at Private, Nonprofit Colleges and Universities: Academic Year 2013–14." Accessed April 23, 2013. Available at http://www.naicu.edu/special_initiatives/affordability/about/.

National Survey of Student Engagement (NSSE). *Promoting Student Learning and Institutional Improvement: Lessons from NSSE at 13—Annual Results 2012*. Bloomington: Indiana University Center for Postsecondary Research, 2012.

Need Blind Admissions Policy Focus Group, Wesleyan University. "A Brief Statement of Our Stance." May 26, 2012. Available at http://needblindfocus .group.wesleyan.edu/2012/05/26/a-brief-statement-of-our-stance/.

Nelson, Libby. "Money for Military, Not Poli Sci." *Inside Higher Ed*, March 21, 2013.

Office of the Governor of Virginia. "Governor McDonnell Asks College Presidents and Boards to Help Limit Future Tuition Increases." Press release, April 18, 2013. Available at http://www.governor.virginia.gov/news/viewRelease.cfm?id= 1778.

Ohle, Jack. "8 Steps Letter to the Faculty." February 13, 2013. Available at https://docs.google.com/document/d/1cJtgNrvoK4dOI7SGLAngXJUKLi2GoXD kJ3Hjwt7oKY0/edit?pli=1.

Olds, Kris. "On the Failure of Legacy Governance at the University of Virginia." *Inside Higher Ed*, June 15, 2012.

Ollman, Bertell, *The Ideal of Academic Freedom as the Ideology of Academic Repression, American Style*. New York University Educational Project. Accessed November 6. 2013. Available at http://www.nyu.edu/projects/ollman/docs /academic_freedom_content.php.

Oppenheimer, Mark. "For Duquesne Professors, a Union Fight That Transcends Religion." *New York Times*, June 22, 2012.

"Penn State's NCAA Sanctions." *Washington Post*. Accessed November 6, 2013. Available at http://www.washingtonpost.com/wp-srv/sports/ncaa-sanctions -penn-state.html.

Pierce, Susan Resneck. "Lessons from Virginia." *Inside Higher Ed*, June 18, 2012.

Provence, Lisa. "Bad Form? BOV Ignored Own President-Replacing Precedent." *The Hook*, June 15, 2012.

Ratcliffe, Caroline, and McKernan, Signe-Mary. "Forever in Your Debt: Who Has Student Loan Debt, and Who's Worried?" Urban Institute, June 26, 2013.

"Responses to President Sullivan's Resignation, Part 3." *University of Virginia Magazine*, June 24, 2012.

Ritter, Dowd. "Letter to Birmingham Southern Family," n.d.

Rivard, Ry. "Duke Faculty Say No." *Inside Higher Ed*, April 30, 2013.

Rivard, Ry. "EdX Rejected." *Inside Higher Ed*, April 19, 2013.

Rose, Joel. "Cooper Union Students Fight for Freedom from Tuition." National
Public Radio, June 10, 2013. Available at http://www.npr.org/2013/06/10/190427
334/cooper-union-students-fight-for-freedom-from-tuition.

Rosenberger, Bill. "Access to Marshall Finances Debated." *Herald-Dispatch*
(Huntington, WV), June 15, 2013.

Sack, Michael. "Thank University Trustees Who Voted Against Tuition
Increase." Accessed November 6, 2013. Available at http://forcechange.com
/25263/thank-university-trustees-who-voted-against-tuition-increase.

Safran, Gabriella, et al. "Letter from Stanford University Division of Literatures,
Cultures, and Languages Faculty to SUNY-Albany President George Philip."
October 10, 2010. Available at http://sunyundersiege.pbworks.com/w/page/3189
3408/DLLC%20Stanford%20Letter.

Schonfeld, Zach. "Wesleyan Alumni Voice Opinions on Shift from Need-Blind
Admissions." *USA Today College*, February 14, 2013.

Sizemore, Bill. "University of Virginia Board Reinstates President." *Virginian-Pilot*
(Norfolk, VA), June 27, 2012.

Spector, Harlan. "Part-Time College Faculty Fight for Better Pay and Working
Conditions." *Plain Dealer* (Cleveland, OH), May 26, 2013.

Star-Ledger Staff. "Kean University President Stays Put After Board Shows Confidence in Leadership." *Star-Ledger* (Newark, NJ), February 15, 2012.

State Higher Education Executive Officers Association (SHEEO). "State Higher
Education Finance (SHEF) Report for FY2012 Released!" Press release, March
6, 2013. Available at http://www.sheeo.org/news/state-higher-education-finance
-shef-report-fy2012-released.

Street, Steve, Maisto, Maria, Merves, Esther, and Rhoades, Gary. *Who is Professor "Staff"—and How Can This Person Teach So Many Classes?* Center for the Future of Higher Education (Cefhe), August 2012. Available at http://www.insidehighered.com/sites/default/server_files/files/profstaff%282%29.pdf.

Stripling, Jack. "Disappearing Departments." *Inside Higher Ed*, May 7, 2010.

Stripling, Jack. "Teresa Sullivan Will Step Down as UVa's President After 2 Years in Office." *Chronicle of Higher Education*, June 10, 2012.

Sullivan, Teresa. "Statement to the UVa Board of Visitors." *Chronicle of Higher Education*, June 18, 2012.

Thornton, Saranna, and Curtis, John W. "A Very Slow Recovery: The Annual Report on the Economic Status of the Profession, 2011–12." American Association of University Professors (AAUP). Accessed November 15, 2013. Available at http://www.aaup.org/file/2011-12Economic-Status-Report.pdf.

Toppo, Gred, and Schnaars, Christopher. "On Line Education Degrees Skyrocket." *USA Today*, August 7, 2012.

Travis, Scott. "FAU Trustees Criticize President's Handling of Incidents." *Sun-Sentinel* (Fort Lauderdale, FL), April 16, 2013.

United Faculty of Florida-Florida Atlantic University Chapter. "FAU Faculty and Students Rally Against Slashed Summer Course Schedule." April 11, 2011. Available at http://www.uff-fau.org/?tag=florida-budget.

Veiga, Alex. "Phoenix Closing 115 Locations." Associated Press, October 16, 2012. Available at http://www.businessweek.com/ap/2012-10-16/university-of-phoenix-closing-115-locations.

Wilson, Robin. "The New Faculty Minority." *Chronicle of Higher Education*, March 18, 2013.

Wood, Carol S. "Rector Dragas' Remarks to VPs and Deans." *UVA Today*, June 10, 2012. Available at http://news.virginia.edu/content/rector-dragas-remarks-vps-and-deans.

Worland, Justin. "FY 2011 Budget Deficit Climbs." *Harvard Crimson*, November 4, 2011.

Index

If you enjoyed this book, you may also like these:

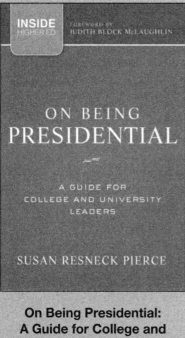

On Being Presidential:
A Guide for College and
University Leaders
by Susan Resneck Pierce
ISBN: 9781118027769

Confessions of a
Community College
Administrator
by Matthew Reed
ISBN: 9781118004739